MY SHORT
(but exciting)
TIME WITH THE
MILITARY

MY SHORT
(but exciting)
TIME WITH THE
MILITARY

Don Paul

Order this book online at www.trafford.com
or email orders@trafford.com

Most Trafford titles are also available at major online book retailers.

Printed in the United States of America.

ISBN: 978-1-4669-1063-8 (sc)
ISBN: 978-1-4669-1064-5 (hc)
ISBN: 978-1-4669-1065-2 (e)

Library of Congress Control Number: 2012900057

Trafford rev. 01/24/2012

 www.trafford.com

North America & international
toll-free: 1 888 232 4444 (USA & Canada)
phone: 250 383 6864 ✦ fax: 812 355 4082

TABLE OF CONTENTS

Chapter 1

HOW IT ALL BEGAN . . .

112ᵀᴴ BOMB SQUADRON (LIGHT)—
OHIO AIR NATIONAL GUARD

In September of 1947, at the tender age of 17, I enlisted in the Ohio Air National Guard for a three-year stint. It really wasn't something I had a burning desire to do but one of my high school friends, Paul Mason, had a friend in the Air Guard who had put a bug in his ear about joining up. As a result about a half dozen of us joined for the adventure of it with the promise of a few bucks in our pockets every three months. I believe at that time a Private's pay was about $90 a month so our pay amounted to roughly $3 a day so every three months I got a check from the state of Ohio for $27. That was quite a bit of money in 1947.

All we had to do was attend weekend meetings once a month and go for two weeks of training once a year. It sounded good to me since I had always been a nut about airplanes. As it turned out what had driven Paul's friend to recruit us was the $25 a head finder's fee he got for getting us to sign on the dotted line for the three years!

Since the Air Guard was having a recruiting drive at the time, we were promised an airplane ride as a reward for signing up. They had quite a

Paul Manson & I with Paul trying on an Air Force B-4 flight jacket. One of the 112th Bomb Sqdn. B-26 Invaders being parked. New recruits being given a flight in the Guard C-47 over the Cleveland, Ohio area. I'm the sixth in line in the right row.

photo session because one of the squadron pilots, Chuck Tracy, was also a reporter for the Cleveland Press. A bunch of us were taken out to the airport and given a sight seeing ride over Cleveland in a C-47 Dakota fondly called "The Gooney Bird." (The C-47 was the military version of the venerable Douglas DC3 used by most of the airlines prior to WWII.) That was a real thrill for me since it was my very first airplane ride.

For that flight we were all issued ill fitting parachutes which we were told to get fitting tightly by adjusting the straps. If, in an emergency, we had to bail out of the airplane a bad fit on the straps, when the parachute opened, would give you an instant change of voice! I can still picture the pilot, a Major, telling us that in case of an emergency he would sound the warning horn. When the horn sounded the third time we had all better be out of the airplane or we would be following him out!

It was all a great adventure for me and I was immediately hooked on flying. We all had our picture taken in the airplane which appeared in the Cleveland Press. Paul Mason and I had our picture taken, with me helping Paul don a flight Jacket. This picture also appeared in the paper which was another thrill.

The 112th was equipped with Douglas A-26 Invader light bombers, real hot rods for their day. The aircraft designation was subsequently changed to B-26 when the original Martin B-26 Marauder was phased out of the Air Force inventory. The 112th was based at Cleveland Airport in one hanger in the southwest quadrant of the field. I believe those hangers still exist today. When I enlisted I thought I would go in for being a crew chief on one of the B-26s. As it turned out I was talked into going into the armament section of 206th Air Service Group which was attached to the 112th. We took care of the .50 cal machine guns and turrets and anything else concerning the armament on and off the aircraft. Actually this was fine with me since I also liked guns.

Our monthly weekend meetings started out on Friday evening and ran from about 7PM to 10PM. On Saturday our day started at 8AM and ran until about 6PM. Sunday they took it easy on us starting at 8AM and running until about 4PM. We were taught a lot about the military, both good and bad, by the men in the squadron that had served in WWII. In the armament section we learned all about the workings of the .50 cal. machine guns and the turrets in the B-26's they were mounted in. We learned to field strip the guns and reassemble them correctly. We also learned how to clean and oil the guns, which is really important for proper function, especially in the very low temperatures encountered at high altitudes. Safety was also a prime subject when handling these weapons.

Our commanding officer in the armament section was Lt. Albert Jacquet, soon to become Captain. He had served in the armed forces during WWII. He was really a fine officer and gentleman and took us "under his wing" teaching us about all aspects of being responsible and safe armament men. We also had some great NCO's (noncommissioned officers) in the section that also gave us fledgling armament people the benefit of their experience.

The B-26 had, for its time, a unique system for controlling the two rear turrets on the aircraft. The gunner sat in a compartment located behind the bomb bay. In that compartment was a periscope, not unlike that found in a submarine, that extended vertically through the top and bottom of the plane and was capable of swivelling 360 degrees. The gunner sat on a swivelling seat, similar to that on a tractor, that was mounted on bearings in the floor of the compartment and also could swivel 360 degrees. On the body of the periscope, mounted about halfway up from the floor of the airplane, was the eyepiece and a little bit below that were the handles that controlled the turrets and the guns. As the periscope was turned, both turrets followed in azimuth and as the handles were rotated the guns in the turrets followed in elevation. If the control handles were rotated up the gunner saw out of the top of the periscope and the guns in the upper turret rotated in elevation and the gunner could see his target above. By the same token when the control handles were rotated down. The gunner saw out of the bottom of the periscope and the guns in the lower turret rotated in depression and the gunner could see his target below. For its time the system was novel. I know this seems pretty "windy" but I don't know how else to explain how the system worked.

When it came to our uniforms, they were issued to us out of the inventory that they had on hand. Most of this stuff I believe was being recycled from the leftovers from WWII. As usual there were just two sizes, too large and too small! Luckily I had an aunt who was a "cracker jack" seamstress and she tailored all of the clothing I got and made me look like a million bucks. I even asked her to tailor my fatigues but that is where she drew the line!

One of my chums, Don Durey, did become a crew chief and I tagged along with him on many of the flights in the B-26s. He had a favorite pilot, name of Tom Tector, a First Lieutenant, who just loved clouds. Around the Cleveland area there was never a shortage of clouds because of Lake Erie. We would take a B-26 up and play tag with them. Flying in those days was no where near as restricted as it is now.

Since the B-26 was a bomber and I was just baggage I could pick where I wanted to sit for the flight. My favorite spot was up in the Plexiglas nose section, which normally held the Norden bombsight, where the visibility was essentially unrestricted. When we were up buzzing the clouds, it was really thrilling!! Sometimes Tom would race in toward the base of a towering cumulus and at the last minute pull up and climb up over the top of it. In the pull up we would probably pull two or three Gs and when we got to the top of the cloud, and he pushed over, we went into negative Gs. Sometimes he would zoom left or right around the cloud base. We just had a great time and I loved every minute of it.

Many times we made night flights and I remember going up to the Niagara Falls area to circle around and see the lights on the falls. On one night flight I was located in the rear gunner's compartment. As we circled over the city of Buffalo, NY, in order to see the sights better, I switched on the power to the turrets and began slewing them around and running the guns up and down as I viewed the sights through the periscope. In not too long a time there came the order, over the intercom, to stop fooling around with the turrets since as they rotated the guns acted like small rudders and the pilot was tired of correcting the airplane to compensate. So much for my fun!

Occasionally we would fly east into Pennsylvania and note the twinkling lights on the mountain tops with a slight curl of smoke coming up. Those were probably illegal stills, or at least we thought so at the time.

I recall one time Tom said he had a cousin who ran a gas station down in Cincinnati and wanted to go down there and see if he could find it from the air. We found it all right. On this flight I was up in the nose of the airplane. Once Tom had the station located we made a circling turn and descended while picking up speed. We made a low, and I mean LOW, altitude pass which really means we buzzed the place! I recall factory chimneys being higher than we were and when we passed over the gas station I could swear I saw a guy pumping gas, looking up with his jaw hanging open. We couldn't have been more than a couple hundred feet in altitude and going like a bat out of hell, with those big radial engines roaring!! That was fun, and probably dangerous as well, but when you are young the danger aspect really doesn't enter your mind.

I can recall being involved in only one "legal" buzz job. There was an air show somewhere in Ohio and I guess the 112th had been requested to stage a "flyby." I was in one B-26 of a flight of three or four B-26s, led by Col. Kelly that made the flight. It was a beautiful flying day and once we found the field we made a pass, low and fast, in formation right down the center of the field. I had a "grandstand seat" sitting up in the Plexiglas nose of one of the trailing Invaders. I'm sure the folks at the air show enjoyed our buzz job as much as I did.

Another time we were down over southern Ohio just boring holes in the sky when a P-51 from one of the local squadrons showed up off our right wing. He looked us over for a while and then proceeded to do a giant barrel roll right around us. That was quite a maneuver!

Here is one I'll never forget. Again we were up poking holes in the sky somewhere between Buffalo, NY and Cleveland. It was a beautiful sunny day with puffballs of clouds roaming about the sky. Off in the distance in front of us our pilot, Tom Tector, spotted an airliner, a Martin 404, at a little lower altitude, and probably also heading for Cleveland. Tom was always a lot of fun to fly with and he had friends flying for the airlines that were always bragging to him about how fast their Martin's were. I guess they had the same engines as the B-26, Pratt and Whitney R2800's. Anyhow, Tom put our B-26 into a shallow dive to pick up speed and bring us to the same altitude as the airliner as we overtook them. At that point we were at the redline on the airspeed indicator, about 350 mph, and flying probably 150 mph faster than the Martin. We passed them on their right side and just before we overtook them Tom "killed" the left engine and feathered the prop! So we zipped by them on one engine alone! I would have given anything to see the expressions on those pilots' faces when they saw us go buzzing by on one engine! Today if that happened our pilot would have been hung from the yardarm, at a minimum!!

I also recall other occasions that we had some excitement rather than just fun. We were taking off from Cleveland airport, in the evening, and had to line up behind a DC-6. He took off and we taxied into position and held for take off until he was off the runway and airborne. In those days no one even thought about the vortices that came off the wing tips of heavy aircraft at high angles of attack and moving relatively slow as this one was doing. Anyway, we were cleared for takeoff and Tom "fire walled" the throttles and we were on our way. I was sitting in the jump seat situated right behind the pilot and the flight engineer. Not too long after we were airborne, probably 300 or so feet in the air, we ran into one of these vortices and immediately the B-26 rolled up on it's right side. The wings were vertical and I was looking to the right at the trees in Rocky River Reservation! When I looked at the pilot, he was frantically trying to roll the aircraft to the left, but to no avail!! Planes don't fly too well on their sides!! Tom must have had his left foot pushing that rudder pedal through the firewall! It seemed like an eternity before we came out of the turbulent air but we did make it and were flying straight and level again. Whew, that was a close one! I think we all needed a change of underwear after that flight.

Another evening we were coming back from a flight and were landing at Cleveland Airport. Again we were in a B-26 and on short final and Tom turned on the landing lights. He usually held off turning them on because he said he had a tendency to fly down the light beams. Not Good! Well, for some reason we landed long and probably didn't touch down until about half way down the runway. The landing was hot and we were really moving. Tom was standing on the brakes to try and get the airplane slowed down. These planes did not have reversible props to help in slowing down. I could hear the brakes moaning and was watching as the end of the runway was fast approaching! At the end of this runway was the south perimeter of the airport and a fence. On the other side of the fence was the Metropolitan Park and a road that followed the fence.

This was kind of a "lover's lane" where couples liked to park and watch the planes land and take off (or whatever). As I said, I was watching the end of the runway fast approaching. Between the end of the runway and the fence there was an area of about 1000 feet of dirt, gravel, and all weeds. Well, we went off the end of the runway and into the weeds and cutting a lot of them with the wind-milling props. I could see quite a few parked cars because they were lit up by our landing lights, which were like searchlights.

The folks in the cars must have thought we were coming through the fence because all I saw were doors flying open and guys and gals scattering!! I can only imagine what they thought seeing this large airplane coming at them with lights blazing and props thrashing! We must have scared the hell out of them! I know we scared the hell out of us!! We made the turn back to the taxiway with about 200 feet clearance from the fence! Another change of underwear was in order for us and probably for a lot of the folks on the other side of the fence also. Ahhh, the joys of flying.

On one occasion, and one occasion was enough, I had the opportunity to help the mechanics change the spark plugs on both engines of one of our B-26s. Now there are eighteen (18) cylinders on each engine, two rows of nine, and there are two (2) spark plugs per cylinder. If my math is correct that adds up to seventy-two (72) spark plugs. As the plugs were replaced, the threads of each plug had to be coated with an anti-seize grease because of the high temperatures in the cylinder heads. This was done to facilitate the removal of the plugs at the next change. One had to be careful with the grease so as not to get any on the electrodes of the plug, which would cause shorting. Also, each plug had to be tightened to the correct torque and then safety wired in place to prevent the plug from coming loose and being blown out. It was a tedious job, but rewarding. After finishing, the crew chief fired up the engines and they ran like champs! There is nothing quite so sweet as a big radial engine running at high RPM and not missing a beat.

One weekend two of our pilots, I believe one of them was Capt. Stuart Graham, needed some flying time so I was asked, along with my crew chief buddy, to crew the C-47 for them. We left early Friday afternoon and headed down into Kentucky and landed at Fort Knox, the Army tank-training center. The pilots wanted to go to the PX (Post Exchange) there. The Army GI's down there couldn't believe their eyes when they saw us enlisted men talking and joking with these officers. I guess that just doesn't happen in the Army.

After we refueled, we took off and headed East up across Pennsylvania and on into New York state to Mitchell Field. By this time we were into Friday evening and these pilots apparently had relatives in this area so we were left with the Gooney Bird to service and watch over. Being young and adventurous we slept in the C-47, which wasn't too bad. Saturday morning the pilots showed up and we headed home for Cleveland. On the way the weather really turned sour so we landed at Erie, Pennsylvania to sweat out the storm. Apparently it was a slow-moving storm so we had to spend another night in the Gooney Bird while the pilots went to a local motel. This night turned out to be no fun at all. It got as cold as a refrigerator in that airplane with the cold rain beating down on it. We were half tempted to fire up an engine to get some cabin heat but decided against it. Instead we found some greasy old canvas engine covers in the back of the aircraft and rolled ourselves in them. It helped a little. Sunday turned out to be beautiful and we got back home with no further trouble.

One incident that I vividly recall was quite devastating! We had just returned from a flight in a B-26 with pilot Tom Tector and had just taxied into our parking spot in front of our National Guard hanger. Right after the engines were shut down we opened the cockpit canopy and I boosted myself up and was sitting on the top of the fuselage just taking in the view. Our pilot and crew chief were busy with their post flight checklist. Parked right next to us was a T-11, which was a small twin engine navigator-bombardier trainer from the Air Force reserve that had the hanger right next to ours. For some reason both of it's engines were running at high RPM. As I watched, the side door in the fuselage opened and out jumped one of the crew. He proceeded to duck under the trailing edge of the left wing and forward toward the left engine. All I can assume is that he came out to pull the chocks from under the wheels. I heard a very loud "POP" like someone opening a Coconut. The whole side of that airplane immediately turned red with blood! I guess the pilot saw what happened because the engines immediately shut down. The next thing I heard was the thin wail of the siren from a meat wagon (ambulance) which shortly came screeching to a halt in front of this aircraft. I really couldn't see what happened next but I assume they took this unfortunate fellow and headed for the closest hospital. From what I saw it appeared that this individual was dead. They did leave behind one guy whose distasteful job it was to go around with a canvas bucket and pick up bits and pieces of the victim's brain and skull. Shortly thereafter a crew showed up with a fire hose and hosed down the parking area and the T-11. I don't think I have ever seen so much blood! It took a while for the trauma of that incident to sink into me. Then it took me weeks to get it out of my head.

Chapter 2

SUMMER CAMP # 1

OUR FIRST TWO-WEEK summer camp was in September of 1948 and the whole squadron moved to Atterbury Airstrip which was part of Camp Atterbury close to Columbus, Indiana. I don't remember just how we got there, quite possibly by train. I do know that the motor pool, all our trucks and other vehicles, went from Cleveland, OH to Columbus, IN by caravan. I remember being out on the strip watching some of our B-26s' arrive. I was out close to the runway watching this one pilot make his approach and the first thing he touched down was the nose wheel! There were some officers standing close by and I heard one of them exclaim, "ground that guy, whoever he is!"

This really was the first totally military experience for a lot of us and as I recall was kind of exciting. We got to experience that "good Army chow" and some of the other distasteful aspects of military life, such as KP duty (kitchen police) and guard duty, (with an unloaded gun, naturally!) We got to load ammunition and bombs into the B-26s' and some of us got over to the range at Camp Atterbury to watch the pilots make their strafing and bombing runs.

One night in the "chow hall" our mess Sgt. came walking through asking what we thought of the food, we had Steak that night. All I

Bomb Squadron Here Begins Combat Training Mission

1948 - ATTERBURY AIR STRIP
COLUMBUS, IND.

WORKING ON A LOWER gun turret at the Atterbury Army Air Base are Pfc. Don J. Paul and Pfc. Ken R. Klein.

INSTRUCTING Corp. Roger Ramm on an upper rear gun turret is Lieut. Al Jacquet.

By CHARLES L. TRACY
Aviation Editor

ATTERBURY AIR BASE, COLUMBUS, Ind., Sept. 25.—Flying two missions daily under simulated combat conditions, the 112th Bomb Squadron of Ohio's Air National Guard from Cleveland Airport, is whipping itself into fighting trim at this abandoned air base in the heart of Indiana.

Here for two weeks of intensive field training on rigid wartime schedules, 170 Greater Clevelanders are learning what makes an air base tick.

They've already proved that an air unit as well as an army moves on its stomach and that the squadron cook is key man in putting those planes aloft on time. Lagging operations the first few days were traced directly to the cooking.

Transporting a complete mess isn't as simple as moving a squadron of planes. Today everything runs smoothly as it must for morning flight crews have but a scant two hours before the afternoon hop gets under way. From 5:30 a. m., when Sgt.

Harry Pryor arouses the camp with a whistle, until 5:30 p. m., they're zipper-up in flying togs.

After that it's a short evening of letter-writing, comradeship in the makeshift officers' club and post exchange, or at the base theater where there's a different movie every night. Lights go out at 10 and there's little interest in nearby Columbus, a town of 14,000.

group which maintains the planes said today that they were satisfied with the results achieved thus far in the unit's first full-time maneuvers.

Fifty per cent of enlisted personnel are 17 and 18-year-old youngsters without previous military experience.

*   *   *

A controline model airplane contest will be staged at the Mansfield Airport Sunday, Oct. 3. The competition will be a free-for-all with trophies awarded the first three places in the A, B, C, D stunt and jet divisions.

Maj. Lloyd M. Griffin, commanding officer of the squadron, and Maj. Robert A. Kelley, commander of the 206th service remember hearing were a lot of complaints about the tough meat, and rightfully so, it was like trying to eat shoeleather! All he had to say about that was that the chewing was good for our teeth and gums. Couldn't fault him there.

There also happened to be a skeet range at the airstrip and being the armament section we just happened to have with us a half dozen Winchester 20 gauge shot guns. The shotguns were equipped with Cutts Compensators on the barrels. We also had a whole bunch of 20 gauge ammo. With the Compensators we could set up the shot guns for a 6-inch pattern to a "manure spreader" and everything in between. When we weren't busy on the aircraft we were blazing away at clay pigeons at the skeet range. Unfortunately hearing protection was not even thought of in those days so I probably came away somewhat hearing damaged in my left ear. I know at the time I couldn't hear out of that ear for the best part of a week. All in all it was a good experience for me and I enjoyed it.

Our First Sgt. at that time was a fine gentleman by the name of Harry Pryor who had spent a lot of time in the service during WWII. Sgt. Pryor was a prince of a man and gave us "still wet behind the ears" GI's a lot of good advice, especially concerning the "girls" in town when we got our weekend passes. I for one will never forget him.

Chapter 3

SUMMER CAMP # 2

OUR SECOND SUMMER camp was in July of 1949 and took us to Dover AFB (Air Force Base) in Dover, Delaware. We traveled by train and I got to see a lot of the countryside, especially in Pennsylvania, that I had never seen before.

The base at Dover was much larger than Atterbury Airstrip that we had been to the previous year, and is located very close to the Atlantic Ocean. We got busy right away since this was purported to be an intense two weeks of training. There was going to be a lot of air to air gunnery using the turrets in the B-26s' giving the gunners much needed practice. They would be shooting at target sleeves towed by other aircraft. Along with that there would also be bombing, strafing, and rocketry to give the pilots their simulated combat practice.

We, the Armament Section, immediately went to the ammunition dump and withdrew thousands of rounds of .50 caliber ball ammunition along with many "Blue Whizzer" bombs and lots of 1.75-inch rockets. The Blue Whizzer bombs are about the size of a 100 lb. fragmentation bomb but are just made out of sheet metal and painted blue, hence the name Blue Whizzer. The bomb is filled with sand, to give it some weight, and a smoke cartridge is placed in the tail to mark where the bomb impacts

After 5 Years, Clevelanders Test Bombing Eyes

By CHARLES TRACY
Aviation Editor 1949

DOVER, Del., July 2.—"Blue whizzers" rained down on an island target in the Atlantic today as the Air National Guard's 112th Bomb Squadron sharpened its bombing eye on two weeks of full-time duty.

Dropping sand-filled 100-pound-ers from their Douglas B-26 Invaders speeding 280 miles an hour at 10,000 feet, flight crews had their first actual bombing practice in five years.

Lieut. Robert (Peggy) Faulhaber, Brecksville insurance man in civilian life who holds both navigator and bombardier ratings, scored a direct hit on the 20-foot shack in the center of the target, despite his long lay-off from the bomb sight. Faulhaber navigated the formation to the target on Ship Shoal Island off the coast of Maryland, and dropped the first bomb.

Breaking into trail formation, planes carrying bombardier-navigators were switched to automatic pilot, giving the men at the sights complete charge of guiding them over the target. Pilots of planes without bombardiers toggled their bombs on signal from the leader.

Made up of Clevelanders, the 112th, commanded by Lieut. Col. Lloyd M. Griffin, shared this abandoned Air Force base with three Ohio fighter squadrons of Brig. Gen. Errol H. Zistel's 55th Wing. The general, who lives in Bay Village and his wing staff

Capt. Tracy

BOMBING UP with "blue whizzers" (above) are Sgt. Carl Lamparter (left), of 1921 Maynard Ave.; Pfc. Joseph H. Kasper, of 2191 Clarence Ave., Lakewood, and Corp. Donald J. Paul, of 4221 W. 50th St.

ARMAMENT CREW (above, right) loads 50-caliber ammunition into nose guns of a B-26 for a strafing mission. Shown here are Sgt. Richard W. Knapel (left), of 2851 Alpine St., and Sgt. Carl Lamparter, of 1921 Maynard Ave.

from Columbus are here for the training session.

Bad weather during the first week limited operations and sent the bombers scurrying on long-range missions to Florida, Alabama and South Carolina so as not to lose valuable flying experience. On their return Lieut. Al Jacquet, armament officer, and his men rushed loading of bombs and machine gun ammunition.

While today's bombing scores were not too impressive, Lieut. Faulhaber said the mission greatly improved flight crew teamwork, so essential to "hitting a pickle barrel from 20,000 feet."

Gunners of the crews have their day tomorrow when they fire the plane's four automatic turret guns at giant sleeves trailed behind tow-target planes flying over the ocean. Rocket firing and operational readiness tests, in which the bombers will try to evade the fighters, are on the schedule before the units return to Cleveland tomorrow afternoon.

JOE KASPER

BARRACKS AREA - DOVER AFB
DOVER, DELEWARE - JULY '49

KASPER'S CAR

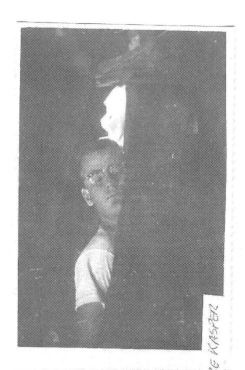

MORE KASPER

FRIENDS "BLUE WHEEZERS" WITH BAND - GEO, GFELL, ME, KEN KLIEN, KASPER

CARL LAMPHARTER

ME WITH .50 CAL
MACHINE GUN AMMO

?, Me, Capt. Jacquet, ?

Don "Jelly Belly", ?

JB, ?, Me, Chuck Gutnovitch

Joe Kasper

FLIGHT LINE - DOVER AFB
B-26 INVADERS

KASPER

MUTT & JEFF

B-26 "ROO"
REMAIN OVERNIGHT

ME & REWKLEW

ENGINES RUNNING &
READY FOR A MISSION

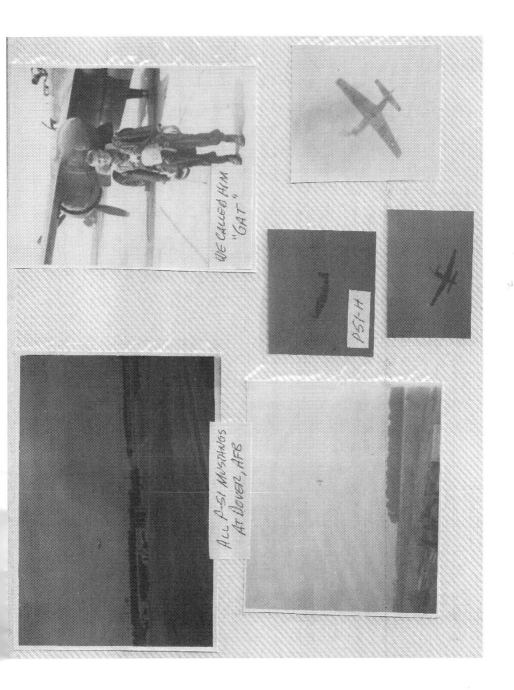

WE CALLED HIM "GAT"

P51-H

ALL P-51 MUSTANGS AT DOVER, AFB

giving the bombardier a visual fix on where his bombs hit. The 1.75-inch rockets were just that, 1.75-in. in diameter and sported a dummy warhead. They were mounted on rails on the wings of the aircraft.

What we didn't know at the time was that the .50 cal. ammo had to be specially prepared for the aerial gunnery. We in the armament section were in for a real treat! The ammunition came in sealed cans inside wooden boxes, as I recall about 100 belted rounds to the can. These small belts we then fastened together to form 400 round belts. Once we removed the ammo from the cans it had to be color-coded so the gunners could identify their hits on the target sleeve. This was done by dipping the tip of each round in a heated mixture of beeswax and a color, be it red, blue, green, or yellow. Needless to say this was a real pain in the butt since the weather was warm and humid and the color mixtures had to be kept heated in flat shallow pans while we dipped the bullet tips. We dipped and dipped until we all looked like we had been in a paint fight! Each aircraft would be firing one turret, which had two guns. Each guns ammo cans held about 400 rounds of ammo making 800 rounds required for each aircraft and as I recall we had at least 12 aircraft and multiple missions were scheduled. That is a lot of ammo to be colored!! We spent many days on this task alone. In our spare time we filled and loaded Blue Whizzer bombs into the aircraft along with mounting the rockets on the wings so the pilots and bombardiers could get in their flying and practice.

Then one day a "bad thing" happened. One of the aircraft came back with a rocket hung up that didn't fire. We removed it and took it into the shop to see what the problem was. I guess it was the firing squib that was bad. And then someone said, "lets take it apart and see what makes it tick," so we did. We removed the nozzle in the tail and then removed the grain of propellant, which looked like a big piece of licorice about two feet long and 1.65 inches in diameter with four lands running lengthwise on the outside and a hole down the middle for even burning. Then someone said, "let's see if we can get it to fly." So we cut a good chunk of the propellant off the grain, maybe 8 inches, and put it back in the body of the rocket. We also cut off one of the lands to serve as a fuse. At this point we did not reinsert the nozzle. Our armament shop was on the far eastern edge of the field and had a very large drainage ditch, running north and south, next to it close to the perimeter fence. We conned one of our group, Joe Kasper, to go and place the rocket in the bottom of the ditch, leaning against the side of the ditch and pointing skyward. When it was all set he lit the fuse and ran like hell up the steep side of the ditch back to where we were huddled to watch the outcome. Well, there was a lot of fire and smoke but no rocket flight! (Mind you, in this bunch of delinquents were upper three graders from WWII that should have known better, as we all should have.)

Disappointed, we retrieved the now dormant rocket and decided to do it right! We put the remaining propellant grain into the body, after removing a chunk for a fuse, and replaced the nozzle. This time it would be right!

Again, intrepid Joe Kasper placed the rocket down into the ditch, pointed it skyward and lit the fuse. After Joe dashed back to our small group of observers, there was much fire and smoke again but the rocket remained where it was. We waited—and waited—probably a couple of minutes—nothing. The supposed dormant rocket just sat there. Joe, for some unknown reason, decided to go and see what the problem was. When he was no more than 10 feet away the beast came to life and roared up the embankment, luckily not toward him, and must have hit something and went underground! Then it made a sharp left turn, in our direction!! It traveled underground possibly 15 or 20 feet before making a sharp right turn and with quite a roar emerged from the top edge of the ditch and headed skyward toward what we hoped was the Atlantic Ocean!! I think we all went white with fright, I know Joe did. We all had no idea what kind of power that small rocket had!

In no time the Officer of the Day was in our area demanding to know what the hell was going on! I don't, at this point, recall how our NCOs (Non Commissioned Officers) talked their way out of it, but apparently they did because nothing happened to any of us. Whew, that was a close shave and was a subject of closed conversation among us for quite a while.

The next incident was less dangerous, at least for us, and involved the weather. Bad weather had moved into the area and in order for the pilots to get in their flight training time took the aircraft and headed south. They were gone for the best part of a week and by the time they returned it was too late to schedule gunnery flights. So, we took our color-coded ammo, reboxed it and took it back to the ammo dump. Guess what? They would not accept it with the colored beeswax in place. They wanted us to remove all of the color before they would take it back! We went back to our shop and started to do just that. With gasoline soaked rags we began removing all the colored wax from the tips of the bullets. This was about 10 times as bad as putting it on!! Our Armament officer, Captain Al Jacquet, told us to stop what we were doing and stand by. Not only were we getting sick from the fumes, we were in danger of blowing up half the base with all this ammo on hand if we had had a fire.

Cooler heads prevailed and the next day we reboxed all the ammunition and hauled all of it out to the flight line on trailers. We then loaded the boxes of ammo into the aft gunner's compartments of the B-26s'. Each aircraft took about six boxes and they took off and flew out over the Atlantic, opened the bomb bays, and the gunners tossed out the ammo!! One gunner said he almost got a fishing boat! Somewhere out in the Atlantic off of Dover, Delaware there are thousands of rounds of .50 Cal. machine gun ammunition polluting the waters.

One day we must have been in some kind of formation and the 1st Sgt. was going up and down the ranks looking us all over. When he got to me he stopped and really gave me a stern look. I guess the sun was glinting off the peach fuzz on my 19-year-old face. He asked me when was the last time I shaved and I replied that I didn't indulge in that practice yet. He informed me that I had better start and ordered me to get my butt over to the PX and acquire some shaving gear! So started my ritual of shaving, maybe on a weekly basis.

Another incident happened in the shower. A bunch of us were in there trying to get the days grime off our bodies when someone noticed something behind my right ear. Upon closer examination it turned out to be a Tick trying to get fat on my blood! One of the more experienced guys said not to touch it since if it weren't removed correctly I could end up with Tick Fever. I didn't want any part of that! After the shower this same individual said the only safe way to remove the insect was to burn it out by holding a lit cigarette close to it's head thereby causing it to back it's head out. Just pulling on the body breaks the insect apart, leaving the head in place under the skin, which then gets infected and results in Tick Fever. So we proceeded with that course of action. However, the individual performing this operation only had a cigar handy! Any port in a storm, and we got on with it. I thought he was trying to burn my ear off! At one point he said the Tick seemed to stop moving. Well, he kept trying and finally he was successful in removing it. I guess he did a good job since all I suffered was a pretty good burn behind my ear!

Since things were fairly quiet the word was out that weekend passes would be available to anyone desiring one. So three of us, Kenny Klein, Joe Kasper and myself decided to go down to Rehoboth Beach, DE which was not too far south of Dover. The three of us got a room in a dinky little hotel near the beach and spent all of Saturday out on the beach. We just laid around, swam, and tried picking up girls, you notice I said tried.

Anyhow, the sun was pretty intense and after a few, 4 or 5, hours I started to seek out the shade. Both Joe and Kenny were dark haired and spent much more time than I did out in the sun. When we got back to the base Saturday night Kenny was in pretty bad shape. He was one crispy critter! We told him to go and see the medics. They must have anticipated this kind of behavior from the troops and were prepared. He relayed to us that when he got there they told him to strip off all his clothes except his skivvies. They had a big bucket of Mentholatum Rub and something like a wallpaper brush and just swabbed him down from head to foot, skivvies and all, with this grease. He came back to the barracks and just climbed into his rack and stayed there! I guess it did the job because Monday he was back on the line. I'm not sure about these days but then, doing something like that, getting sun burned, was a court martial offense.

Chapter 4

SUMMER CAMP # 3

IN AUGUST 1950 we were sent down to Lockbourne AFB, Columbus, OH to what was to be our last summer camp for a while. For me it was to be my last. This time we were all flown to camp except again the motor pool went by caravan. Since the Korean War had started in June 1950 that was the hot topic of conversation. Were we going to be pulled in? No one knew, and if they did, they weren't saying anything. I don't remember much of that summer camp and I don't know why.

I do remember we took one of the B-26's and with a tug towed it out to a firing butt, which was a big pile of dirt faced with big wooden poles. We loaded up the ammo cans on the lower turret and fired the .50 cal. machine guns over and over again. I know we burned out the barrels on those guns. I guess they allowed us to do this firing because they knew it would be good experience for what was coming. Little did I know.

I also remember going flying one day, which turned out to be rather exciting. The pilots had taken the dual control B-26, this was probably going to be a check ride for a pilot. This aircraft had both the turrets removed. Another guy and I occupied the gunner's area in the rear, which had lots of room because of the lack of the periscope, the gunner's seat, and the lower turret. It probably was a pilot check ride because we did do a lot of

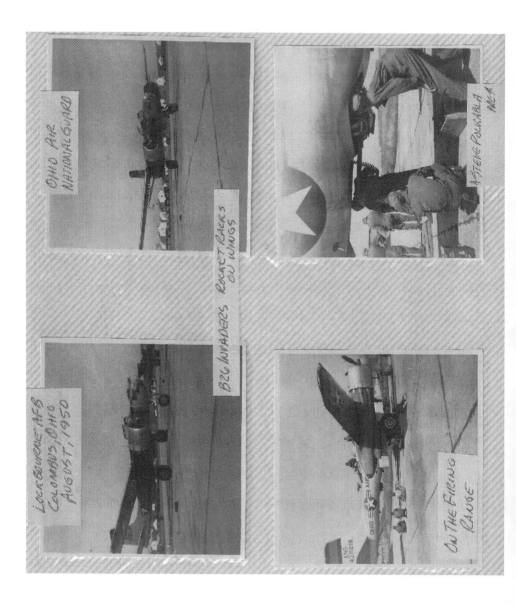

OHIO AIR NATIONAL GUARD

B26 INVADERS ROCKET RACKS ON WINGS

LOCKBOURNE AFB COLOMBUS, OHIO AUGUST, 1950

A-STEVE POKRABLA NEA

ON THE FIRING RANGE

SHOT THE HECK OUT OF IT!

FIRING .50 CAL LOWER TURRET GUNS

KEN KLIEN
GETS DOUSED
BY IKE KASPER

LITTLE DID I KNOW I'D
BE IN THE U.S. AIR
FORCE IN TWO MONTHS!

LOADING "BLUE
WHIZZER" BOMBS

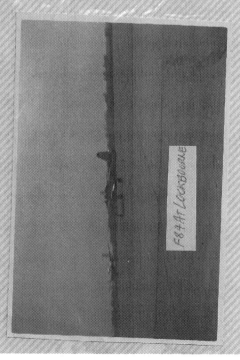

F84 AT LOCKBOURNE

maneuvering. That didn't bother me and I actually enjoyed it. However my companion, Dick Musall, didn't and began to get airsick. I don't know where he got it but he came up with a small plastic bag, which he proceeded to fill. It was a hot day and it really started to get stinky back there! My stomach was starting to rumble just from those nasty fumes. Up in the top hatch of the compartment was a small flap type door, maybe 4 inches X 2 inches, that could be opened for a little air. Dick took his bag of barf and tried to stuff it out that little opening. Unfortunately the slipstream immediately opened the bag and drained the contents in seconds! That was not the worst part. The seals around the large hatch were in bad shape so most of the "liquid" drained back into our little space! Yuk, what a mess!! Somehow I managed NOT to get sick, how I don't know.

Now the real fun began. On returning to the field the pilot found, that when he lowered the landing gear, he was not getting a "down and locked" signal for the nose gear. For the next half hour or so the pilot tried everything he could to get that light to come on, dropping the flaps, diving and zooming, running the gear up and down, to no avail. We finally did a slow flyby of the tower and they couldn't see anything wrong, the gear looked fine. Soooo, in we came and the pilot held the nose up as long as he could and then gently eased it down. The two of us in the back had our "pucker strings pulled up tighter than a bulls ass in fly season," and that's tight! I'm sure everyone on board was in the same situation. But, the nose wheel held and we were down safely. Whew, that was a close one! I guess Dick and I had the job of cleaning up the airplane afterward but we lived through it.

Another bit of excitement for us was we heard some scuttlebutt that a pilot of ours had been challenged to a dogfight between one of our B-26's and a P-51. That sounded like a real mismatch. Anyhow, at the appointed hour we all were out on the flight line to watch this spectacle. The two aircraft were probably up at about 5000 feet and amazingly the B-26 did a fine job of keeping that P-51 off of his tail. There must have been a lot of grunting and groaning in the cockpit of that B-26 with all the gyrations they went through. We were impressed!

When our two week encampment was up we went back to Cleveland and there it was announced that the 112th was being activated and we would become a regular Air Force Squadron some time in September. We would be on active duty with the United States Air Force for 21 months and we were told to go home and get our affairs in order prior to being inducted. I was in college at the time and when I went to school to withdraw they asked if there was anything they could do to get me a deferment and I declined. I guess I was looking for a new adventure and I surely got one!

As with everyone first going into the service I started out with the rank of Private or as fondly referred to as "Buck Ass" Private. That rank entitles one to NO stripes on your sleeve. As time went on and I learned more and more about my job as an Armament Specialist I attained higher and higher rank moving up through Private First Class, one stripe, then Corporal, two stripes, and finally Sergeant or Buck Sergeant. This entitled me to three stripes on my sleeve. Once in the regular Air Force this rank became known as Airman First Class or A/1C. For reasons to become clear later on this was the highest rank I was to attain in the Air Force.

We spent one weekend out at the old Bomber Plant at the Cleveland airport getting our physicals prior to induction. What an experience that was! A slew of doctors spent the day poking and prodding us, looking into every orifice in our bodies, and drawing copious amounts of blood using blunt needles affixed to large syringes. The WAC Captain that drew my blood bound up my upper arm and proceeded to try and insert the so-called needle into my vein. When the needle skidded up my arm the only thing she could say was that I had very tough skin! That was when I turned my head away.

There were quite a few guys in the 112th that had put in a lot time in the service in WWII. Most of them had good jobs, wives and families, and were looking forward to peaceful and rewarding lives. There was one T/Sgt. that had 60 months overseas time alone! When they got into the Air Guard no one had any idea that another shooting war would come along so soon! They either had joined because they liked a smattering of military life or they wanted to hang on and get the retirement benefits. There was a lot of complaining but not much could be done about it. Some did get out in a few months time claiming hardship but that was only a few.

As I recall, in a week or so, we were sworn in and became part of the U.S. military establishment. We were told to report to the Cleveland Union Station, with all of our gear, at a certain time and date for shipment by train to Lawson Field, Fort Benning, Georgia. My short, but exciting, Air Force career was about to begin.

Chapter 5

112ᵀᴴ BOMB SQUADRON(LIGHT)USAF

WHEN 1950 CAME along my enlistment was about up when, on June 25th, things hit the fan in Korea. I was told that I could get out of the Guard but my name would be sent to the Draft Board with a special note attached to it assigning me immediately to the Army and directly into the Infantry. How true this was I have no idea, but I did choose to reenlist. Besides, why should I chance going into the Army as a Private when I could remain in the Air Force as a Sergeant?

When we arrived at Lawson Field, Fort Benning, GA we were still in our summer khaki uniforms. At that time in the service we were told when we could wear our summer or winter uniforms. Our winter uniforms were wool and still the old Olive Drab ones that we had been issued to us in the Guard. One of the things we did, soon after our arrival, was to be outfitted in our new Air Force Blues. We were issued everything, from skivvies right out to a heavy blue "horse blanket" overcoat. This was the first time I had had a complete uniform. There was a tailor on the base, very close to our area, and I have no doubt this man became quite rich with all the work we all sent his way to get those uniforms fitting just right!

FORT BENNING, GA
SEPT '50 TO MAY '51

FT. BENNING OCT
'50 5TILL M.D.'s

GYM AT FT.
BENNING, GA

STEVE, GUS, ME,
JOE

ME, CLARENCE
LUTHER, JOE
KRAMER

REEZE, BOB, SAM,
ME, UNCLE-SACK,
AUNT MARGE, MOM

Life in the regular Air Force was far different than anything I had experienced before. Summer camp did not come any way near to preparing me for this. Our day usually started at 0500 (that's 5am!) with the sounding of Reveille. Our barracks was right across the street from the Headquarters building which had a very large speaker mounted on the roof. When Reveille sounded, which naturally is done using a bugle, we didn't just wake up—we were blown out of our sacks!

Then we performed our "morning ablutions" (talk about chaos in the latrine) and at 0530 we were "invited" outside to partake in morning calisthenics for at least 30 minutes, not that we all didn't need them. Usually while we were out there, grunting and groaning in the pitch dark, a company or so of Paratroopers would go trotting by on the road coming in from their morning 5-mile run! That usually made us feel a little less sorry for ourselves.

Our barracks were two story wooden affairs, from WWII, with two small rooms at one end of the lower floor, for the barracks chiefs, usually upper three graders. The accommodations for the rest of us "grunts" were double stacked bunks, one over the other. Each bunk had a screen type center which was attached to the outside rails of the bed frame with springs making it a little more comfortable then sleeping on the bare floor. Over that screen was a mattress, about 3 inches thick, on which you put your sheets and blanket and pillow. Actually these beds weren't too bad and I don't recall losing any nights sleep. There were probably a total of about twenty of these double stacked bunks, ten on each side of the center aisle, on each floor for a total of 40 men, all sleeping head to toe.

At least once a week, or more often, the First Sgt. would have us "police the area" outside right after calisthenics. We would all go down to the end of our barracks area and line up single file abreast. We would then proceed to walk across the whole area, eyes glued to

Bob REEVES &
ME JAN '51

Bob Hibbins, Dick
MARCANTE, ME,
JOE KASPER, CHUCK
CHITROVICH

LAWSON FIELD —
FORT BENNING, GA

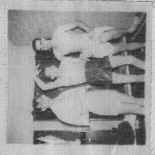

DICK MARCANTE, ME &
JOE KASPER

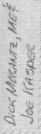

PAUL
DONALD J
AF 23 580 133

- 39 -

ME, BOB REEVES

CHARLEY CVITKOVICH

THE "SCOOP CHUTE" OUR CHOW HALL

FT. BENNING, GA

JOE KASPER, ME

HOME SWEET HOME

KASPER &
BOB REEVES

JOE KASPER &
FIRST LOVE

JOE KASPER, SONNY, ME, ROGER LOWTHER

HAS GOT TO BE JOE KASPER

the ground and pick up any little bit of trash we found, be it a stick or cigarette butt or whatever and made sure it got thrown away properly. When GI's smoke and they are finished normally they don't just flip the butt. It gets "field stripped" which means tearing the paper down the side, scattering the remaining tobacco to the wind and rolling up the remaining paper into a tiny little ball which is then discarded. (Take a look around any Military installation and see how little trash, if any, is lying around.) Then it was back into the barracks at 0600 to make our beds and clean up our areas in preparation for the morning inspection at 0630.

Your bed had to made just right and tight enough to bounce a quarter off of. If your bed wasn't made correctly the inspecting NCO(non-commissioned officer)would tear it up and you had to do it over—until it was done to his satisfaction.

Your clothes had to be hung neatly, and in the correct order, Class A's down to fatigues! Your footlocker, at the end of your bunk, had to have the lid open and everything had to be neatly packed in there. You learned to be neat, or else!

One does learn to hustle rather quickly since if you didn't pass inspection you could get "extra duty" which could turn out to be quite distasteful, at the very least. At 0700 we were off to the chow hall, which was located right behind our barracks. Our workday started at 0800 down on the flight line.

Being in the armed service makes a person appreciate his mother very rapidly. Clean underwear, sox, and clothing in general, which we all took for granted while at home, quickly became a thing of the past. It is amazing how quickly one runs out of these things and I found myself rummaging through my "dirty bag" to find some of these items that were still wearable. I know it sounds grungy but one must have clothing. The rule for skivvies was to wad them up and throw them at the wall. If they didn't stick they were wearable! How about that?

Anyhow, I tried doing my own laundry in the latrine, sox and skivvies, but that was too much of a hassle. I even tried wearing my fatigues in the shower and soaping them down, not a good idea. It took forever to rinse them out! Finally I learned about the base laundry and the small fee they charged for doing this chore. What a God send!

What we had to do was buy a small rubber stamp, which had your initials on it along with the last four numbers of your serial number. In my case DP0133 since my serial number was, and I guess still is, AF23580133. Also we had to purchase a small inkpad for the indelible ink so we could stamp and identify every piece of clothing we sent in. We also sent in our summer khakis but you had to specify how much starch to use, light, medium, or heavy. If one didn't specify they came back like boards! You could hardly get your feet through the legs and the collar of your shirt would almost saw your head off! Again, one learns quickly.

Since we were a National Guard outfit there were not too many lower ranks, i.e. Buck Private (no stripes), Private First Class (one stripe), and Corporal (two stripes). There is always a need for the lower ranks to take care of Kitchen Police or KP as it is fondly referred to. I was a Buck Sgt. (three stripes) and unfortunately that group was put in with the lower ranks to draw KP. KP is not a fun duty! One is usually awakened at around 0400; you quickly dress and make up your bunk, and stumble over to the chow hall where the cooks assign you duties. These duties are usually "dog" work, scrubbing pots and pans and general clean up in the eating area. During and after meals it again is pots and pans along with the trays the GI's used for eating.

Another duty was to sort out the bread. Right after the chow line was a large caged in storage area that was about 10 feet long by 2 feet deep and 6 feet high. On shelves in this cage the bread was stored, all of it white. I guess it was baked in the base bakery and was ordered by the mess sergeant as needed. It was all sliced and tended to grow mildew rather rapidly. It was the KP's job to go through the bread before every meal and throw out all the moldy stuff. Who knows, maybe the cooks saved it for stuffing at Thanksgiving!

Since our chow hall was small we didn't have any fancy equipment to do the pot and pan washing. (i.e. "The China Clipper" a super dish washer that was available in the officer's mess.) What we did have was a large double sink, one for hot soapy water, and one for hot rinse water. Sometimes the guy assigned to wash trays got lazy and didn't change the wash and rinse water often enough and the result was greasy trays. If it wasn't discovered and the greasy trays were left for the next day the guys using them could get sick!

To avoid this and to spur the tray washer to do a good job the Flight Surgeon would regularly make surprise visits to check things out. The trays were stored in a rack right at the door and you took one prior to entering the food line. On one occasion I saw the doctor run his fingers over a few trays and then proceed to dump the whole rack over onto the floor!! Not only was he angry but the GI's coming in for their meal had to wait until the "floored" trays could be washed and re-racked. That was one busy guy doing the washing and you can bet he didn't ever allow his washing and rinsing water to get cold and greasy again.

On KP we usually got some breaks in between meals but for the most part it was a long hard day, which usually ended about 1000 hrs (8pm).

MECHANIC OFFICERS

FLIGHT LINE
LAWSON FIELD
FT BENNING, GA

FLO & I -
IN LOVE!

ATLANTA, GA
ATLANTA/PEURY

DICK VELOTTA, SONNY KASPER,
ROGER LOWTHER, BOB REEVES

I HAD A 27" WAIST -
AT THAT TIME

One duty I didn't mind during KP was peeling potatoes. That was one chore that was mechanized. The "peeler" was a machine that had a hopper on the top about 14 inches in diameter and a foot deep. The hopper had a cover and at the top of the hopper was a water inlet line. In the bottom of the hopper was a motor driven abrasive disc along with a drain for the water and "peelings." To perform the "peeling" one loaded a bunch of potatoes into the hopper, turned on the water, put on the cover, and fired up the motor. The operator was to look into the hopper occasionally to view the potatoes peeled state. When most of the peels were gone the operator was to switch off the machine, remove the potatoes and then proceed to "eye" them by hand. Being a somewhat lazy guy I just left them in there until not one eye remained. I guess that was wasteful but it sure saved me a lot of trouble. I never got any complaints.

One thing I thought was quite odd occurred during the first month or so down at Fort Benning. At night after Taps (lights out), which occurred at 2200 hrs (10pm), and all was quiet in the barracks you could hear a half dozen or so guys sobbing. I guess they were homesick. I never felt that way. It was all just another of life's adventures for me.

Another important time of the day is called "Retreat" and this takes place at sundown. "Retreat" is sounded on a bugle and at that time the flag is slowly lowered. If a person is outside during this time the protocol is to face the flag, come to attention and salute until the last note fades away. One day some of us guys were in the barracks and Retreat started to sound. If you were inside no action had to be taken, just go on about your business. Anyhow, at the first note we heard these running feet pounding on our porch and the door slam open and in comes an officer at full gallop! This phony didn't want to stand outside at attention during that short time. He made a real "good" impression on us enlisted folks!

The first barracks we were billeted in were the good old fashioned two story wooden ones. They were in pretty good shape and were heated by a natural gas furnace. Thank God we didn't have coal as a source of heat! Most of the guys, probably about 40, set up housekeeping downstairs. Since that was full, the overflow, about 15 of us went upstairs. It can get cold at night down in Georgia in the fall and naturally the furnace was turned on. The thermostat was located downstairs and was set at some appropriate temperature, probably 70F. Little did we know that the baffles for the heating ducts were set so that the majority of the hot air was sent upstairs.

Now began "the battle of the thermostat." We were roasting upstairs and the first floor guys were freezing! When it became unbearably hot upstairs someone would go down and turn down the thermostat. Shortly after that one of the frozen ones downstairs would turn it back up!

Naturally heat rises so we were getting a double dose while downstairs got practically nothing. And so it went for most of the first few nights until a couple of the guys almost came to blows. The senior NCO who was naturally in one of the two private rooms DOWNSTAIRS settled this. We were threatened with bodily harm if we came down and touched the thermostat again. The next day one of the upstairs crew and I took a look at the ducting in the furnace room and got it straightened out. "The battle of the thermostat" came to a screeching halt! Whew!

Another duty besides KP was "barracks duty." This chore entailed taking care of the barracks after all the GI's had left for their duty stations for the day. We had to sweep down the middle aisle of both the upstairs and downstairs. Before the guys left for the day each one had to sweep out his area into the middle aisle. After sweeping the middle aisle was then mopped. The floors in our barracks were just wood and as such were all cracked and splintered from constant mopping. That made the job that much harder since the mop caught in all the splinters.

After that was finished the latrine, which was downstairs at one end of the barracks, had to be tidied up. It was usually quite a mess after the guys had gotten ready for the day that morning. As I recall there were 6 or 8 toilets "out in the breeze" (not in stalls), a large trough type urinal, 6 sinks and a shower area. All this for about 55 guys who tended not to be very neat! It wasn't bad duty though. If you hustled the job would essentially be finished by noon and the only other thing to get through was the daily inspection. The 1st Sergeant and usually the Adjutant would come and inspect the barracks to make sure everything was "ship shape." In most cases it was and then the rest of the day was leisure time, reading or writing letters.

Some of the guys in the squadron, not many, were real slobs. None that I recall were from our original bunch from Cleveland. Once a week, in the morning, we had to strip our beds of the linen and turn it in to the supply sergeant for clean issue. On that day all the mattresses were rolled up and put at the head of your bed with the pillow set neatly on top. In the evening, usually after chow, everyone made their beds to get ready for taps. These lazy individuals wouldn't make their beds for 3 or 4 days and would end up sleeping on the springs fully clothed! Needless to say these individuals grew rather smelly. There was one fellow that was threatened by his bunkmates to "shape up." When he didn't comply he was given a "GI Bath." Three or four individuals dragged this guy, fully clothed, fighting and kicking, into the shower, stripped him down and scrubbed him with bar soap and brushes head to foot! I don't recall him being a slob after that action. He apparently got the message.

One or two months after we had arrived at Lawson Field, Fort Benning, someone in headquarters of the 112th found a stash of money left in the squadron slush fund. This money, left over from our days in the Ohio Air National Guard, was normally used for social events. We had had some very good ones in years past. So, it was decided that once again the squadron would throw one last bash using these funds.

A hall was reserved somewhere in downtown Columbus, GA and all the arrangements were made for a real wing ding of a party. Lots of good food and naturally adult beverages were procured and a date was set for the shindig. Unbeknownst to the squadron Padre (at least I think so) some "dancing girls" were also invited. The word was out that these girls would shed some or all of their clothing sometime during the festivities. As a result all attendees were warned that cameras would be strictly forbidden since these girls were a little on the shy side. I had no problem with that since I didn't even have a camera at that point in time.

The date of the party finally came along and we were all bussed into Columbus to the hall for the party. It was quite a mix of enlisted men and officers. Fraternizing between the ranks was allowed for this occasion. As I recall it was quite a bash and we all had more than enough of good food and probably more than we should have had of drink. The troops were getting restless and were itching to get to the main event of the night, the dancing girls.

The venue for the party was more like a gymnasium than a hall. It had something like bleachers along at least one side so we were all afforded a good view of the upcoming festivities. All the tables and chairs were moved away from the center of the floor and we all picked out our spots for the best view. Some of the guys were quicker than the rest of us and got the front row seats.

Shortly the girls "handler" came out and had a few words to say to all these young horny GIs. I do recall that he admonished us all to refrain from touching or grabbing at the girls as they went through their dance routines. As a parting shot he said, "Remember, any one of these girls could be your sister." A very loud GROAN went up from this audience of newly minted airmen in reply to that statement. This guy was in trouble. But one of our officers got the microphone and calmed the troops down.

So with that out of the way the house lights dimmed and the "canned" music was cranked up. One by one the girls came out and performed their routines, which were much appreciated by the gallery. As I recall none of the girls was left with a stitch on at the conclusion of their dances. One thing that did seem odd was that every now and then I would feel a sudden flash of heat. I was too young for hot flashes and attributed the sensation to the viewing of the dance routines. It was only afterward that I learned one of the guys had snuck in a 4" X 5" Speed Graphic camera and was using Infrared film and flash bulbs, thus the "hot flashes" during the performances. I do recall seeing some of those shots afterward and they did turn out quite well. Luckily I was not on any of them. The guys in the first few rows of seats were not so lucky!

There was one guy in particular, seated in the front row of seats that seemed to be particularly mesmerized by the girls. I was watching him almost as much as I was watching the girls. Well, maybe not as much. Anyhow, he almost seemed to be petrified, and maybe some of him was—a little bit. He appeared to not be moving a muscle. The girls were noticing this also and seemed to be playing to him quite a bit. I do recall the one young lady doing her routine directly in front of him and he seemed to be hypnotized by her movements. She was gyrating in her routine and all the time removing bits and pieces of her costume and hanging them all over him. This guy was "locked on."

Finally when it came to the point where she was about to remove her last bit of clothing, covering her bottom, she moved in toward him. He was still not moving at all. He couldn't keep his eyes off this young lady. When she got within about three feet of him she snatched off her bottom and threw her one leg up and over his shoulder. Still no movement from him. Then with one quick swipe of her one hand she caressed her crotch and wiped that hand across his face. That prompted a very loud groan from all the guys in the room and the girl quickly detached herself from her victim and fled the room.

This guy still sat there, petrified, with remnants of her clothing hanging off his head and shoulders. He may still be there for all I know. Hopefully he did not end up with any communicable disease as a result of his experience. He probably had enough alcohol in him to kill any bugs that got transferred in the encounter.

All in all it was a fun time and we all got back to base in one piece. Thank goodness for the busses because a lot of us surely would not have been able to make that drive.

We were one squadron of a wing that was called the 117th Tactical Reconnaissance Wing. The other two squadrons were P-51 outfits, the 157th from Greenville, South Carolina and the 160th from Birmingham, Alabama.

Not long after our arrival at Ft. Benning the Army decided to hold War Games. Since we were a Tac Recon Wing they really didn't have much use for us in their War Games. However, they did decide to use the P-51 squadrons in simulated close air support. Our armament section, for this operation, was designated to help the P-51 outfits. As it turned out we ended up mixing Napalm for them. All we did was mix laundry detergent with gasoline and voila—Napalm. The more detergent you put in the gasoline the thicker the mix. The thin mix gave a very hot, short lived, blast of flame and the thick mix gave a long lasting burn. This really is nasty stuff. How this Napalm got loaded into canisters and then loaded onto the aircraft turned out to be someone else's problem.

Since we were on the Army's air field we had grandstand seats for their air operations. These consisted of air drops, from two to three thousand feet, of all sorts of military equipment. The Army had C-82 Boxcar aircraft into which they loaded anything from Jeeps up to Six by Six 2 ½ ton Trucks and all kinds of artillery.

All this equipment was securely lashed to pallets and had at least one very large parachute affixed to bring it down after it was pushed out the rear of the aircraft. These equipment drops were quite spectacular!

On one drop they pushed a Six by Six Truck out the rear of a C-82. All went well, at first! The truck came out and the three parachutes opened slowing the truck's decent. Then things got interesting. One of the parachutes ruptured and the truck started to accelerate earthward! Then the other two chutes, one after the other couldn't stand the strain and they also tore. Down came this truck, somewhat stabilized in it's fall by the streaming chutes, and struck the ground! It hit fairly flat because of the streaming chutes, but it hit HARD! I swear it must have bounced 10 to 15 feet in the air when it hit! Scratch one truck! For us that was the most exciting part of this operation.

The paratroopers on base also took part in this operation and we later heard that they had lost a few guys in a night drop that missed the drop zone. Very tragic. It only shows that war, games or not, is a very hazardous undertaking.

Our squadron was from Cleveland, Ohio and the other two squadrons in the wing were from South Carolina and Alabama. This turned out to be a potentially explosive combination. One Yankee bunch and two squadrons of Rebels! By the time December rolled around we were on the verge of restarting the Civil War! It was really getting bad!

In spite of this situation we were all anxious about leave over the holidays and the scuttlebutt was that either you could go home for Christmas or New Years but not both. There was a lot of grumbling, naturally, and everyone was trying to figure out which holiday was best for them. Then someone had a real flash of genius and they just sent everyone home for at least 10 days, which took in both holidays.

Everyone was excited about going home for the holidays but we had to figure out how to get there. Luckily the M/Sgt. from armament, Kenny Smith, and his wife were going to Cleveland and offered Joe Kasper and I a lift if we helped out with the gas. We were more than willing! There was one small problem and that was Smitty's car was a convertible and Joe and I naturally got the back seat. It wasn't bad when we started out in Georgia but by the time we got up into Kentucky it was getting darned cold in that "rag top!!" We didn't make any stops and drove straight through. I don't think I had called home and the folks were very surprised and happy when I showed up.

That Christmas was memorable for me because Flo and I went to downtown Cleveland one snowy evening and I bought her a nice diamond engagement ring. We were now officially engaged. It was a wonderful and all too short holiday leave.

All good things come to an end and so it came time to return to Ft. Benning. I was going to take the train but my Uncle Pete said he would pay for airline tickets so that gave me an extra day or so. I can remember the terminal at the Cleveland Airport at that time. It was just a little round affair about 200 feet in diameter, and jam-packed with passengers. That was all there was at that time. What a mess! I remember that I was supposed to go by DC-4 or DC-6 (four engine prop jobs) from Cleveland to Pittsburgh, PA and then down to Memphis, TN and on into Columbus, GA and Fort Benning. The best laid plans—!

At Pittsburgh the winds and turbulence were so bad, almost everyone on board was sick, we had to continue on to New York and then the fun began! I was put on small aircraft and began jumping from one airport to another. I think I was in the air for about 12 hours! When I got to Columbus, GA it must have been 2 or 3 in the morning and the place was shut down. I finally found a cab and got out to the base. I was supposed to report in from leave at 2400 hours (12am) and I was about 4 hours late when I got there. When I checked in I got some nasty looks but that was all, thank goodness!

When I got back to the barracks I had a big surprise. While we were gone they had shuffled all the personnel in the wing and re-manned all the squadrons. No more squadron against squadron, now it was one on one and that totally defused the situation. All our gear had been gathered up and put into one barracks. We also had been assigned to different barracks. What a mess that was trying to sort it all out, but we made it.

I have to mention, in passing, our chow hall. We had to have had the worst cooks in the world! How they could take good food and screw it up like they did was phenomenal! Here is how that came about. When we all got down to Ft. Benning and formed the wing I guess we were heavy on motor pool personnel and light on cooks and bakers. The military solution to that problem was obvious, take some of the grease ball mechanics and decree they are cooks. Voila, the problem was solved. The GI's had to suffer for that solution. However, I can't say I lost weight as a result of this situation. Sometimes it was tough to gag down the food, but one must eat. Breakfast was probably the best meal of the day and I packed away at least my share. One of my favorite breakfast dishes was SOS. (That's GI for S—t on a Shingle) It is supposed to be creamed chipped beef on toast but in our case it was creamed hamburger. The worst meal we had to endure was dinner on Sunday. They gave the cooks time off so the meal consisted of cold cuts, cheeses and bread. We fondly referred the cold cuts of meat as "Horse c—k." Leave it up to the GIs for colorful phrases.

One thing that did seem odd to me was that all the cooks were buying cars, which were scarce in this area and expensive. I found out much later, when I was in Korea in fact, that the cooks had been taking the good food into town and selling it. I heard they had gotten caught and sent off to prison "to make little ones out of big ones," otherwise known as hard labor.

All our cooks turned out to be from the south and as a result we got Hominy Grits as a side dish for almost every meal! If you don't know what "grits" are the best explanation I have is "bee bee's in white sauce." (And they taste about the same) I must have thrown away enough grits to cover the state of Georgia to a depth of 6 inches! To this day I can't look grits in the face without feeling a little queasy.

Occasionally we would get tired of the mess hall food, or maybe the menu for that meal wouldn't be too enticing, so we would go to the local branch of the PX (Post Exchange) and have a light meal of burgers and fries. It was a change of pace. They also had a "Juke Box" there which had all the latest hit songs in it.

We also had an Airman's Club where we could go and relax at night and have a few beers and shoot pool or whatever. These facilities were usually pretty nice and quite comfortable.

Every now and then everyone runs into some kind of a medical problem. One day I found that a filling had fallen out of my one front tooth, a gold filling at that. So one morning, after chow and checking in with the First Sgt., I trundled off to the local sick bay. Since the Air Force didn't have it's own medical facility I went to the one run by the Army, which in this area took care of mostly paratroops. (One had to go through the local medics to make an appointment to see the dentist.) Here I was, feeling sorry for myself having to go to the dentist when I entered this medical building. I was not prepared for what met my eye. There was a whole bunch of young GI's in all states of disrepair. Broken arms, broken legs, broken heads, these guys were really in bad shape! I guess being a paratrooper does have its hazards! Anyhow, I made my appointment and in a few days reported to the dentist's office on the main base. I was going to see the Air Force dentist since the Army had his or her own. Why this arrangement, I have no idea.

I again was feeling sorry for myself having to undergo this ordeal. In the waiting room there were about 6 or so Army guys, none of which were over 18, waiting to see the Army dentist. One by one they were taken into their dentists office and when they came out their jaws were already pumped up with Novocain. When they had all reappeared they were all trying to tell each other, through numbed mouths, how many teeth they were losing. Most were losing 3 or 4 teeth and some of them a whole lot more! I guess these kids were from the hills and had never seen a dentist in their lives, until now.

The male receptionist was a real sadist! He had a chalk box about half full of teeth and came out and rattled it in front of these poor GI's faces telling them that they were going to substantially add to his collection. What a jerk!

I began to feel much better about my situation. I finally went in to see my dentist and after a little anesthetic and some drilling I was ready for a new filling. The dentist then asked me what kind of filling I would prefer. Since the old one had been gold naturally that is what I said I wanted. His reaction to that was as if I had slapped him! He then said, rather loudly, "What the hell do you think this is, Fort Knox? Either you get silver or porcelain, take your pick." I quickly chose the latter. Luckily I had no serious health problems while I was in the service.

One of the fellows in the barracks, that I remember particularly, was from Birmingham, Alabama. This guy was "two sandwiches short of a picnic" in the mental department. He was nice enough but really short on gray matter. He would always get his wars mixed up. Like one time I asked him when the battle of Bunker Hill was fought and he swore that is was during the Civil War.

He also had a penchant for going into town and getting drunk. Invariably when he did so he, for some unknown reason, would get a tattoo. I can remember him waking up on a Saturday morning, terribly hung over, and exclaiming "Oh no, not another!" Sure enough there on one of his arms would be another UGLY tattoo. I don't know where he got these things but they were all ugly, badly washed out colors and usually quite fuzzy. Not well defined like most tattoos are. He had one really ugly one on his left forearm. It was a dagger about 10 inches long with a snake wrapped around it. It was green and blue and yellow and in the body of the snake was the name "Moe." I asked him who Moe was and he answered that that was his wife's name! It was short for Maureen. She must have really appreciated that! Wow!!

This same individual was always bragging about his "Hot Rod" that he had back in Birmingham. He claimed he was having it "Souped Up" by a mechanic friend of his. We were always giving him a bad time about this fictional vehicle of his, which he never brought to the base. It was always being worked on, he claimed. One Monday morning he showed up with his pride and joy. It was a '37 Pontiac straight 8 and not in bad shape. When he lifted the hood the only thing we could see that was any different from any run of the mill Pontiac was a shiny finned coil mounted on the side of the block.

We were all snickering over all the work he had done to make this vehicle a fast car. Either this so-called mechanic was "hosing" him or this guy was lying. So we asked him to show us what his car would do. Since we were prodding him unmercifully he, in a huff, jumped in and fired up the engine. The road we were on was just behind the chow hall and was a tar road covered in gravel. There would be no slipping and sliding on this surface! Anyhow, after starting the engine and with the clutch disengaged he proceeded to floor the accelerator until the engine was screaming! Then he just dumped the clutch and—BANG—NOTHING!! He was sitting there, hunched over, clutching the steering wheel, engine screaming, and going nowhere! What had happened was when he dumped the clutch the one U-joint, at the transmission, couldn't take the load and just sheared! All of us guys almost died laughing and as I recall were doubled up and rolling on the ground. This poor guy was sooooo embarrassed. We never heard any more about his "Hot Rod."

While on duty during the day we were always required to be in uniform be it fatigues or class A's. Our fatigues at that time were olive drab coveralls that were functional but ugly. "In uniform" meant wearing a "cover" (hat) also. Class A's were our dress uniforms which in the summer were khaki's, shirt and pants, with a tie, which got tucked into your shirt front, and a cap or Garrison hat. In the winter the class A uniform was our "Blues," a light blue shirt, blue tie, dark blue wool trousers, dark blue wool blouse, (a long jacket) and overseas cap or garrison hat. When outdoors it was required to wear your cover or you were "out of uniform" and subject to a DR or discrepancy report, which went back to your headquarters. This could subject you to a reprimand and extra duty. Fortunately I only got one of those DR's, which resulted in extra duty cleaning windows in the orderly room for a day.

When entering any building you were required to "uncover," or take off your hat. That kind of etiquette is sorely lacking these days and you can see men and boys entering restaurants and never removing their hats, even while eating! Didn't Mom ever tell them?

A lot of my friends couldn't wait to get off the base at night; they donned their civvies, and went off to Columbus or over the Chattahoochee River, which is the state line between Georgia and Alabama, into Phenix City. I was unaware of it at the time but Phenix City was pretty wild! I guess there was gambling to be had over there, among other things, but we were told if we gambled that we had better lose!! I guess they had pulled more than one GI out of the Chattahoochee, face down, that they assumed had won at gambling. I avoided that place.

Anyhow, I was in love up to my eyeballs and had no desire to go roaming. As a result I always had plenty of money and in some cases the "bank" for some of my buddies. Some of the guys that served as "banks" were not as friendly with their loans as I was. If a guy wanted to borrow say $10 from one of these "sharks" he had to pay back $20 on payday! That is called "Usury" and is a court marshal offense. I can remember more than one payday, we were paid in cash, when some of these guys that borrowed heavily would get their pay and turn around and start down the pay line paying off the money he had borrowed. In some cases they ran out of money before they paid off their debts! Not very good! Some of these guys were really in the hole, but they kept doing it.

Actually there were a lot of things to do on the base to keep us occupied and out of trouble. Up at the main base there was the Main PX that had everything in it that a well-stocked department store would have. There was also the Commissary where you could buy food at very reasonable prices. There was a movie theater showing current films, a beautiful big indoor swimming pool, that we used quite often, along with a nice gym and basketball court. We also made good use of the library, so there was plenty to keep us busy.

Since Flo and I had gotten quite serious about one another I decided to take a step toward making our relationship tighter. She was raised Catholic and I was raised outside of any formal religion so I decided to take Catechism lessons at the Catholic church on the base. So that kept me busy at least one or two nights a week.

Fort Benning, as are all large military facilities, was and is a small city unto itself and my stay there was quite pleasant. I didn't know that there were rumblings out there that were about to change that.

Now, here I was, an armament man in a photo recon outfit. Not exactly a good situation. Kind of like "Tits on a Boar Hog." We did work on modifying some of the B-26's to RB-26's by removing the rear turrets but this was really a job for a manufacturer with all the weight and balance and other modifications that had to be made. We were doing "make work" just to keep us busy. I recall one day we weren't very busy and I got tired just sitting around. In the hanger where we worked, in one corner, there was an area that looked like an elevator shaft. Inside it was a ladder that went up to a platform, up about 25 or 30 feet, accessed by a hatch. I climbed up there and lay down to take a snooze. I was about to nod off when I heard someone coming up the ladder. I glanced over to the trap door and as it opened up I was looking at the CO (Commanding Officer)! He just looked at me and went back down. I thought my goose was cooked! I never heard a word about that incident. Why, I don't know.

We did a lot of marching and we got a lot of classroom training in our chosen specialties. We all did get out to the firing ranges and qualified on the M1 Carbine. It was funny; the word was going around that if you got a good score with the M1 you would be shipped immediately to Korea for infantry duty. Some of the guys were firing into the ground in front of them to keep from hitting the target! They got their butts chewed if they got caught doing that. And then there was always at least one guy that would get a jam and swing around with his rifle to report the jam!! A lot of people "hit the dirt" when that happened.

Speaking of marching, since we did quite a bit, we got good at it. I think we had two or three "reviews" while down at Fort Benning. A "review" being squadrons of personnel marching to a military band and "passing in review" for the base commander. That was thrilling to me and I enjoyed it. There were always two or three guys in the squadron that really didn't know their left foot from their right. If you have ever seen a group marching you can always pick out the people that are out of step. They "bob" up and down like "Kewpie dolls." After our first review these individuals were given lessons in marching in order to get them to march correctly. I can remember the 1st Sgt. giving them lessons in between the barracks shouting, "left, right, left, right" and getting nowhere. These guys just couldn't get it! So the only thing left to do was to try and bury them in the middle of the marching group and hope for the best. It really was quite frustrating for the "higher ups."

During one of many phone calls to Flo, it was probably sometime in April of '51, she mentioned the possibility of coming down to Columbus, GA to visit. I thought that was just a great idea. She said she would be coming down for about four or five days and that she would be bringing a friend with her. I told her to make her plans and I would arrange for a hotel room in Columbus.

So in not too long a time she and her friend Mary flew into the Columbus, GA International Airport, such as it was, and from there went to the hotel I had arranged for them. It was wonderful to see her again and, as I recall, I was able to borrow a friends car and also get some of my friends as dates for Mary.

We did hit some of the "night spots" along Victory Drive, which is the main road connecting Fort Benning to Columbus, for dining and dancing. In any of these places there were always plenty of GIs that wanted to dance with our women. As I recall I always turned them down. We just had a

FLO'S VISIT TO
COLUMBUS, GA &
FT. BENNING WITH
FRIEND MARY
DVORAK MAY '51

Flying Home To Cleveland, OH From GA. Me On Leave Prior To Reporting To Langley Field, VA

Oor Last
Picnic — For
A While

great time during their visit and I was able to get Flo on the base to show her where I lived and worked.

At the end of their visit I was able to get some leave time so we decided to fly home to Cleveland. Mary left a day or so early to go back home. Flo and I packed up and went out to the Columbus, GA airport and traveled up to Atlanta and then on to Charlotte, NC by DC-3. In Charlotte we switched aircraft so our flight home to Cleveland, OH was on a big four engine Lockheed Constellation, fondly called "Curvaceous Connie", a very nice airplane for it's day. My stay in Cleveland was a short one and before I knew it I was back in good old Fort Benning, GA.

In February or March of '51 a TWX (telegram) came into our headquarters asking for men in my AFSC (Air Force Specialty Code) to be shipped out to other squadrons in need of that specific code. I was told that my squadron wanted to hang on to me, so they arranged for me to take a test to have my AFSC upgraded, which I did.

That saved me for a while. The next time a similar TWX came in, probably in May '51, all the loopholes had been closed and my goose was cooked. I shipped out the latter part of May '51 to Langley Field, VA and the 154th Fighter Bomber Squadron of the 136th F/B Wing, became my new home for the next twelve months or so. So began a new chapter in my Air Force career.

Chapter 6

154TH FIGHTER/BOMBER SQUADRON, 136TH F/B WING LANGLEY FIELD, VA

IN EARLY JUNE of 1951, after saying adios to the 117th Photo Reconnaissance Wing, at Lawson Field, Fort Benning, GA, and after a delay en-route of about 10 days in Cleveland, Ohio, I reported in to Langley Field, Virginia to the 154th Fighter Bomber/Squadron of the 136th F/B Wing. This was an all Air National Guard Wing equipped with Republic F84-Es, made up of three outfits. Two from Texas and one from Little Rock, Arkansas. The 154th was from Little Rock. The other two squadrons, the 111th and the 182nd, were both from Texas. The wing was shipping overseas in mid June and going to Japan to take part in the Korean War which was going full tilt at that point in time. As a result I didn't really get to know any of my squadron mates very well.

At Langley I ran into an old buddy of mine from high school, Steve Polkabla. He had been in the 112th also and had transferred out. In the line of conversation it came out that I was shipping out to the Far East and I guess his situation at Langley was bad enough for him to volunteer for the 136th.

Since Steve and I were both from Cleveland, Ohio we talked about getting a weekend pass and hitch hiking home, which we did. We really had to hurry since we were due to ship out soon. Steve had a buddy that wanted to tag along so one fine Friday afternoon we three headed out, bound to Cleveland, OH from Virginia.

Here is the amazing part of our journey. Not far from the base there we were on the side of the road with our thumbs out. We weren't there very long when a lone driver stopped and asked us where we were going. Our reply was "Cleveland, Ohio." Amazingly he said that's where he was heading. How about that for luck? This fellow had probably picked us up so he would have someone to talk to on his journey. Not long after we boarded his vehicle we all fell asleep! So much for his having company!

True to his word this gentleman got us to Cleveland and dropped us off. What a stroke of luck this was for us. Anyhow, we split up and went our separate ways. I had a short but wonderful weekend in Cleveland with the family and especially with my betrothed, Flo. How I got back to Langley I don't recall but get there I did.

At Langley one thing was readily apparent to me and that was the food here was quite an upgrade from what I had been used to at Lawson Field. When I expressed my opinion on how good the chow was all I would get were queer looks from my mess mates. They thought it was awful! If they would have had some of the chow I had down at Lawson Field I think their opinions would change, drastically! Also the barracks at Langley were multi-level brick structures with tile floors, again another upgrade. Really quite nice; however, I didn't get to enjoy them for long. In mid June we were loaded on a troop train along with all our gear and we headed for the West coast.

I recall one of the young NCOs (Non-Commissioned Officer)from the 154th bidding adieu to his teary, newly minted wife. He was maybe twenty years old at the time and she was probably just out of high school. He was surely trying to sooth her by telling her he wouldn't be gone too long. I'll have more to say about this couple later in the narrative.

The train's destination was Camp Stoneman, California which was the POE (Port of Embarkation) for the Far East, Japan and Korea. That train ride was really something and I thoroughly enjoyed it. Not only that, it didn't cost me one cent! The Pullman cars we had on that train must have been from the Civil War era. They were really old, but in retrospect if we had gotten anything new they would have been trashed by us GIs anyhow by the time we reached our destination. At least we each had a bed to sleep in every night, made up by the porters.

There were some of our troops on that train, not many, that never drew a sober breath from the time we left Langley until we were very close to the West Coast. I guess these were some of the guys that had been in WWII and did not want to be where they were or to be going overseas. Hence, the alcohol fog. The trip took four days and I was fascinated by it all. I had never been West of Chicago so it was all new to me and I enjoyed it immensely.

Some of the troops on board were very enterprising. At our infrequent stops they would leave the train and buy candy bars, pop, and beer by the case and stow it away. When the mess car ran out of these items, and it invariably did, these hucksters would go into action selling their wares for whatever the traffic would bear, usually $1 to $2 per item. As I recall that was at least four or five times what they cost back in 1951. Good old American free enterprise!

To the best of my recollection our route was from Langley, Virginia up to Columbus, Ohio and then across to Indianapolis, Indiana. From there we proceeded South Westerly to St. Louis, Kansas City, Topeka, Denver, and Salt Lake City. From there we traveled across Nevada, and down into

California to Camp Stoneman at Pittsburgh, CA, which was just East of San Francisco. (I don't think the camp exists any longer.)

Going across Kansas, I was surprised by the flatness of the terrain. In Colorado I was amazed by the Rocky Mountains. I think we passed very close to Aspen, CO where someone said the Mountain Troops had trained during WWII. In Nevada I was struck by the starkness of it all.

When we were about twelve hours from our destination the commanding officer came through the train, looking his troops over, and told anyone that was drunk or unkempt that they had better "shape up" and clean up by the time we arrived at our destination or he would have them arrested and thrown in the stockade! Shape up they did! Some of these guys had been in a stupor for four days and looked like they had been outside crawling around in the dirt! I have seen bums that looked in better condition.

When we got off the train at Camp Stoneman, we were lined up and marched to our temporary quarters. Our route took us right past the stockade and I could not believe how many GIs were behind that barbed wire! The place was packed!! They were all shouting obscenities at us along with epithets like "we'll be here when you come back in a box" and things like that, not very good for our morale. I can only assume that these troops were deserters, having no desire to go to Korea.

I think we spent about a week at Camp Stoneman housed in good old wooden two story barracks. I remember one of the busiest areas on the base was the line of telephone booths that were available to us. There must have been about six or eight phone booths and there was always a line up of about 10 guys waiting for each booth. I assume most of the calls were to home. I think the phone company made out like a bandit just from those few phones.

Then one day, we were told to pack our gear. We were put aboard busses and transported across San Francisco Bay to Travis Air Force Base. Here we received our last shots, for Japanese "B" Encephalitis (sleeping sickness). The medics here were real jokester. As we approached the infirmary there was a small table at the door with a very large syringe having a very large needle attached, and it was stuck into the table! Also On the wall was a small plastic container holding a standard size syringe and needle; however, the needle had been bent to resemble a fish hook! I guess this was meant to emulate the old saying that they gave you your shots with a "square needle with a hook on the end."

After receiving our shots they loaded us onto C-54s for the first leg of our trip to Japan. As I recall these aircraft were owned by an airline called "National Overseas Airways." They were still outfitted like a military aircraft.

If you have ever been on a military C-54 you know that the accommodations are not exactly plush! The seating is made up of Aluminum frames with Nylon cross webbing for support. The webbing is not very flexible and in not too long a time ones fanny was NUMB! There were some women on board, probably WAFs, that served us our in-flight meals which, as I recall, were "C" rations. Not exactly Filet, but edible. These women spent most of their time catering to the officers on board.

We flew from Travis AFB for about twelve long hours, with those four radial engines droning along (thank goodness!) and arrived in Honolulu, Hawaii around midnight. When we deplaned, it was absolutely beautiful! There was a full moon with lots of puffy clouds in the sky and the smell of flowers hung in the warm humid air. If there was ever an urge to go "over the hill" (go AWOL-Absent Without Leave) it had to hit then. We were taken into the terminal restaurant area out on an open patio where we were fed. The food was quite good as I recall and most of us had a few drinks. It was great. The time spent there was only a few hours and off we went again on our second twelve-hour leg.

This time the destination was Wake Island. If you have ever been there you wonder how they ever found the place! It is just a speck out in the middle of a vast ocean with no other land in sight, even from altitude! As I recall, it is an atoll 90% of which is under water. The part that is above water consists of two chunks of land at about 90 degrees to each other. The one strip holds the runway. The other, slightly larger strip, holds the living quarters, maintenance hangers and parking areas. The highest point on the island is 18 feet above sea level. How the Marines defended this place against the Japanese invasion, during the first days of WWII, is beyond me.

On our final approach to Wake I remember looking out the window and seeing props and chunks of aircraft strewn alongside the runway and sticking up out of the sand, probably left over from WWII. Along the shoreline were four or five half-sunk rusting hulks of ships that looked like they were shot full of holes.

We deplaned at high noon and was it hot and humid!! We almost melted. Again we spent our short time there being fed. Afterward we had a little time to look around and there were some Japanese tanks and other vehicles left over from WWII. I couldn't believe how small and dinky these vehicles were! It looked like they were shot full of holes just from rifle fire.

We then re-boarded our aircraft and off we went again on our last twelve-hour leg, destination Haneda AFB, Japan which is very close to Tokyo.

When we landed at Haneda the local time was about midnight and we again deplaned and were hustled into the chow hall to be fed. We didn't spend much time here since we still had another leg to travel, down to Itazuke Air Force Base, close to the city of Fukuoka, on the southern island of Kyushu. That was one bumpy ride and unfortunately I was located in the very rear of the airplane and came very close to losing the meal I had just eaten.

At last, here we were at our final destination in Japan, for the time being. It had taken us roughly thirty-six hours of flying time to get here. Today the flight time is about one third of that, and much, much more comfortable.

ON MY WAY TO LANGLEY FLD VA & THEN TO JAPAN

LANSON FIELD FORT BENNING GA

ENTRANCE MATSU FUKUOKA JAPAN JUNE '57

BASE I STARLING MATSUME JAPAN JUNE '57

WRANGRIZED TENT

Chapter 7

THE 154ᵀᴴ F/B SQDN. AT ITAZUKE AFB, FUKUOKA, JAPAN

WE HAD ARRIVED at Itazuke AFB in southern Japan in late June 1951, after a long flight over the Pacific Ocean. That first night in Japan was actually rather scary for me. When we landed at Itazuke it was very early morning and still quite dark. The air base, which we called "The Strip," still had no accommodations for us so we and our gear were piled into 2 ½ ton or 6x6 trucks (so called because they had six wheel drive) and taken to Base 1, which was about 5 miles away. The crazy nuts from Little Rock, AR, that were driving the trucks, decided to race and there we were, side by side, careening down this pitch black two lane road toward who knew where. Luckily we did arrive safely and were billeted in "Winterized Tents." A winterized tent is nothing more than a wooden frame made of 2x4's with a wood floor and a tent thrown over it and had one or two "pot bellied stoves" inside for heat. I remember there being eight cots in each tent all along the sides and one end.

THIS IS WHERE the scary part came in for me. I had visions of sleeping in my "rack" and some Japanese outside cutting the tent and slitting my throat! WWII had not ended that long ago and I thought there might yet be some fanatical Japanese around that were still angry about losing the war! At the time I wasn't aware that when the Emperor said that it was over, it was over, and all the people had obeyed him.

SINCE THE BARRACKS and chow hall at The Strip were not yet ready for us we slept and ate at Base 1. This meant traveling back and forth about four times a day. The road that we had traveled that first night was just a two-lane dirt road lined on either side with rice paddies and farmers houses. Needless to say the trips back and forth were through some very smelly air that was the result of the rice paddies being fertilized with "Night Soil," otherwise known as human excrement, and this was July and quite hot! I remember one of the guys, Pete Stull, had some real trouble with lunch since by the time we got back to the chow hall on Base 1 his appetite was gone. I imagine he had the same trouble with supper. Luckily for him this situation only lasted about two weeks because he was skinny enough as it was. When our barracks were finally ready, we shipped over to the strip permanently.

One other thing I need to mention about our multiple daily sojourns up and down that road. There were many peasant homes that we would pass but one in particular had the "Benjo" (out house toilet) right out in front right adjacent to the road. There was no door on this "One Holer" and on occasion, when we were roaring past, the same old Mama San (she looked to be at least 100) would be sitting in there smoking her pipe and relieving herself and we would all go nuts hooting and hollering at her. She must have thought we were all crazy!!

The mess hall at Itazuke again turned out to be quite good, at least I thought so. It seemed as though the further away I got from that original mess hall down at Fort Benning the better the food got. Could it be that I was getting used to it or worse yet developing a taste for service chow? On Sundays the cooks would even cook your eggs on a griddle just the way you wanted them. First class!

One of the guys liked his eggs almost raw! As soon as they touched down on the griddle he wanted them in his tray. Talk about sunny side up, these eggs were actually snotty!! However, if anyone said anything about his eggs, like "Look at those eggs wiggling and jiggling" or "Boy are those eggs snotty," that was the end of breakfast for him and he couldn't eat. Some Sundays we took pity on him and didn't say a word.

The one thing that I didn't like in the mess hall was the reconstituted milk, which had an odd taste to it. As a result I started drinking coffee and have done so ever since. The orange juice also tasted like it had gasoline in it. Maybe they mixed it in the same GI cans that they used to clean parts in. I guess it was OK. No one ever died of it that I know of.

The barracks at Itazuke Air Base, or The Strip, were finally finished and we moved from Base 1 to The Strip permanently. The barracks at Itazuke Air Base, which by the way is now Fukuoka International Airport, were one story "H" shaped affairs with bunks lining the walls in the vertical legs of the "H" and the latrine and showers in the horizontal section. One thing that really struck me about the latrine was the location of the urinals. They were on the walls as usual but were located about half way up my shin just below my kneecap! I'm not a really tall guy, 6', so the Japanese that were in flight training here were very short folks. (Our understanding was that this was the Kelly field of Japan and toward the end of the war Kamikaze flight training took place here.)

Outside, all the barracks were surrounded with sand bags piled about waist high. I guess things got a little tense here right after hostilities broke out in Korea. Right down the street from the barracks area was the mess hall and not far from there was the flight line.

Every barracks had a "houseboy" or "housegirl" to take care of the chores usually taken care of by the GI's in the States. They swept up, cleaned the latrine, and took care of laundry and any other tasks they were

JAPAN, JULY '51

MARION KARECKI,
CURTIS PITTARD

TOM MENNELLA,
N.Y.

asked to do. As I recall we didn't pay them very much but they seemed happy to get what little they did. We had it quite easy there.

One day in the barracks, prior to going down to the line, I was combing my hair and noticed my comb seemed to have a head of hair all it's own. Also, my fatigue cap seemed to be lined with hair. So began my "balding process," which today has resulted in enough space on the top of my head for another face!

At The Strip there was also a small "beanery." It was run by Japanese and served snacks to the GI's such as hamburgers and hot dogs and cokes. When we tired of the chow hall fare, we would go there to eat. I had been there a few times and I was sure the cook's name was "Dozo" because when I would ask for a hamburger the Japanese girl behind the counter would always shout out "One hambaga, Dozo." I finally got the flash that "Dozo" meant "please" in Japanese.

The 154th Armament section was housed in a couple of large tents on the flight line right behind where our F-84s were parked. The early missions flown by the 154th were mostly high fighter cover for bombing missions flown by B-29's out of Okinawa, as a result there was little activity involving bombs and rockets. The aircraft carried auxiliary fuel tanks on the bomb racks for most of these missions to give them the extended range required for bomber escort duty. When the aircraft returned from these missions many of them had fired their machine guns fighting off the Migs (Russian fighter aircraft) that had attempted to attack the bomber formations. This is where the "fun" began for me. I had no idea how parochial these National Guard units could be. I had heard from regulars, that had come into the Guard outfit I was with at Fort Benning, complaining of their treatment, but it never registered with me.

In my opinion the armament section of the 154th was badly organized and as it was fleshed out with "outsiders" it became highly polarized. There

OUR BARRACKS AT "THE STRIP"
ITAZUKE, JAPAN

SAND BAGS ARE FOR
BOMB PROTECTION

SWIMMING AT BASE 1
ITAZUKE, JAPAN

CHOW HALL AT
ITAZUKE, JAPAN

BUFORD HARDIN

were the guys from Little Rock and then there were us, the outsiders, the regular Air Force personnel and an occasional ANGer like me.

We, the armament section, essentially were used as a labor pool, at least the "outsiders" were. When aircraft came back from a mission and had fired their guns, our armament chief, Jim Turner, a Master Sgt. from Little Rock, would assign whoever was at hand to service them. In my case I was ALWAYS assigned to empty the spent brass from the holding bins under the four nose guns in the aircraft. This was accomplished by me sitting in a large wooden crate affixed to the top of a bomb dolly and dragged down the flight line by another airman, in most cases Marion Karecki a T/Sgt. who had been in WWII. He would pull me under the nose wheel well of the aircraft and I would open the bins and the spent brass would rain down on my head. There were no specific people assigned to any one aircraft. I don't recall any of the Little Rock personnel being assigned to spent brass duty. It would have been different if the two of us had other armament duties to perform but such was not the case. I began to complain loudly and often that my talents were not being properly utilized, and not necessarily in those words. It didn't take long before the upper echelon in the armament section labeled me as a "trouble maker" and, unknown to me, decided to move me elsewhere. I was about to find out how difficult and painful it is to fight "City Hall."

In early August I was notified that I had been reassigned from the Armament Section to permanent CQ (Charge of Quarters) for the squadron. This was somewhat of a blow to me but I decided to tough it out. My duties were to be "Acting First Sgt." from 6pm to 6am every night seven nights a week. When they said "permanent" they meant it! I was to check all the barracks on an hourly basis for fires and take care of any other problems that arose during the night, and also not sleep during those 12 hours. I was supposed to sleep during the day which turned out to be impossible due to the constant turmoil in the barracks. At night

I got to be "Father Confessor" to all the drunks that wandered into the barracks from town or the local enlisted mens club.

I do recall one of the guys from Little Rock, an upper three grader, a Tech. Sgt., was so enthralled with a Japanese woman, that he was "shacked up" with in Fukuoka, that he contemplated divorcing his wife! They must have been married for quite a while since they had three or so kids. He actually wanted to marry this prostitute. What a jerk!

This is where I can pick up on the sad saga of the young airman from Little Rock, AR and his newly minted wife. Since I was on permanent CQ, and the only phone that could be used to call "Stateside" was in my office, I was privy to snippets of his phone conversations. As it turned out this poor guy got word that his young wife was not about to sit around twiddling her thumbs and wait for him. I guess she was out dating and doing the town while he was gone. I think on a weekly basis this guy would phone Little Rock, AK and talk to his wife for at least an hour, trying to convince her to act like his wife! These calls must have cost him a small fortune! I'd be willing to bet they cost in the hundreds of dollars. How successful he was in this endeavor I really have no idea.

This CQ duty was really was a first class s—t detail. I had no real authority, so in cases where there were problems my choices were to wake the 1st Sgt. or call the Air Police, a no win situation for me. I put up with this duty for about three weeks. One morning, after CQ duty and while still bleary eyed, I went to see the Squadron Adjutant. I told him of my plight and asked to be reassigned back to the flight line in the armament section. He listened patiently and finally, after I was done talking, he asked me if I really knew how much the higher ups in the armament section hated me. I told him I didn't care since I couldn't put up with the CQ detail much longer. He told me to go back to the barracks and that I would hear from him within the next few days.

RICE PADDY - PHEW!

MAIN GATE GUARD SHACK - ITAZUKE

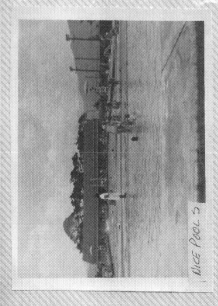

NICE POOL 'S

MAINGATE - THE STRIP - ITAZUKE - COMING BACK FROM BASE I SWIMMING

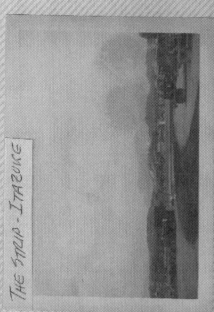

THE STRIP - ITAZUKE

ITAZUKE TOWER

True to his word he called me back in within a few days and told me he had gotten me back on the line and to report for duty in the armament section the next morning. He also warned me to keep my sarcasm to a minimum and my nose clean. I thanked him for his effort on my part and assured him I would, indeed, keep my nose clean.

The next morning as I was walking past our armament tent on the line, just prior to reporting in, I overheard some words drifting through the canvas walls to the effect "that blankity blank Don Paul was coming back down to the line." The four letter words were really flying and I don't recall "love" as being one of them! It looked like I was in for some real "fun."

I may have had some little effect on the structure of the armament section due to my previous bitching. It was no longer just a labor pool. They had broken the squadrons' aircraft down into flights of four planes per flight and assigned individual airmen to each one. This was a much better situation and I got my own airplane to take care of as far as the armament systems were concerned. My spirits lifted immediately and my disposition got positively "sunny".

The F-84 I was assigned to was not in the best of shape, as far as the armament systems were concerned, but I got busy and had it back in tip top condition within a few days. What I thought was really funny was the fact that if one airplane on the flight line got its armament systems inspected it was mine. We had a T/Sgt. in the armament section, by the name of Don McDonald. He was the Armament Inspector for the squadron. He and I initially were like a cat and a dog, always going at one another. He went over my airplane with a fine tooth comb on every inspection but never found anything wrong. A funny thing though, by the time we were ready to ship over to Korea, we ended up very good friends.

The armament section really had it "cushy' in Japan. We had a crew of Japanese personnel, most of which were ex-army, that took care of the .50

C-54

B-26's

PBY

ARMAMENT AREA -
IJAZUKE

JAPANESE WORKERS - THEY
CLEANED THE MACHINE
GUNS FOR US

NME, JOHN PIERCE

caliber machine guns for us. When an airplane came back from a mission, and had fired its guns, all we had to do was pull the six machine guns out and take them into the maintenance area where the Japanese crew took over. They would disassemble them, clean them, oil them, reassemble them, set the head space, and return them to the individual armament crew chief for reinstallation in the aircraft.

I recall the "Papa San" (supervisor) of that bunch was an older gentleman that said he had been a Colonel in the Japanese army and had been in on the Japanese conquest of Korea. His favorite story was about when they would capture a Korean village. The first order of business was to pick out 10 or 15 Korean men from the village, put them against a wall, and gun them down! This was to show the town's people that they meant business and would stand for no monkey business on their part. Very brutal! They surely knew their way around the machine guns though.

With this new organization I was as "happy as a clam." I did my job and got along just fine with most everyone.

The squadron then started to fly missions other than Bomber Escort. Since we were a Fighter/Bomber outfit, we started flying "interdiction" missions to North Korea. These missions were to bomb the supply routes and slow and hopefully stop the flow of war materiel from very northern Korea to their units fighting at the 38th parallel where the fighting had stalled. At this point I assume that the decision was made to move the 136th Wing over to Korea where the aircraft would be much closer to their targets. Our destination turned out to be K2 (the Korean airfield designator) at Taegu, Korea.

We were in Japan from late June 1951 until Mid September 1951. It was not all work for us, even though we were on duty seven days a week, since Fukuoka was just a short bus ride from the air base. I clearly remember the first time I rode the bus into town. I was just getting off the

Wing Tip Fuel Tank

FS-367

I Took Care Of All
Armament Systems On 367

FS-367

FS-367

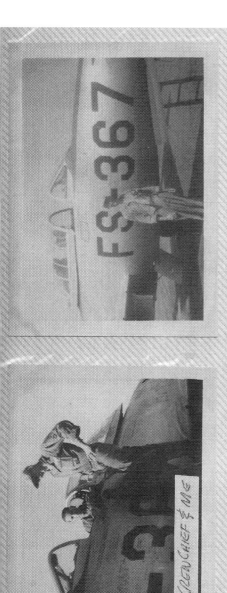

367's CREW CHIEF & ME

260# FRAG
BOMB ON RACK

5 IN ROCKETS

OFF ON A MISSION

FS-395

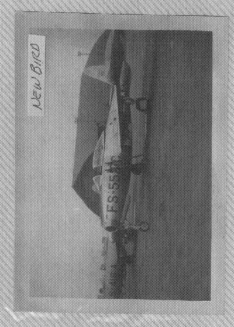

NEW BIRD

FS-554

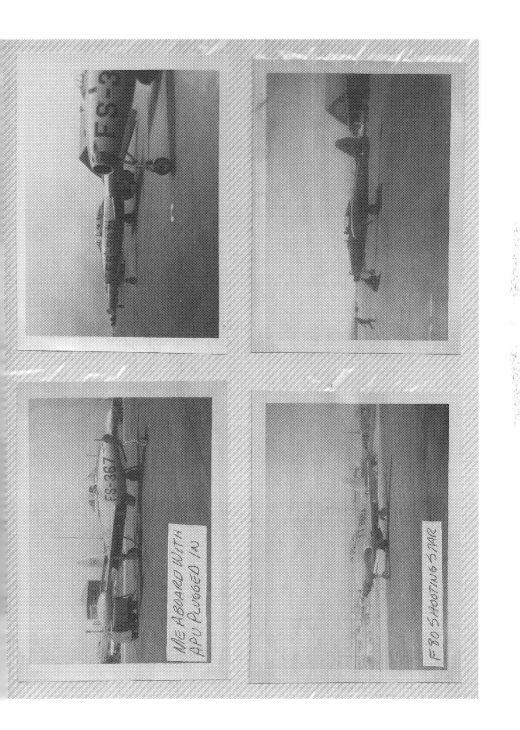

ME ABOARD WITH APU PLUGGED IN

F 80 SHOOTING STAR

Tom Maxwell & Bill Harris

bus when I heard a female voice from a doorway near by, "Hey glassy boy (no doubt referring to my glasses) where you go?" Believe it or not I just hustled off and went about my business shopping.

Fukuoka was an interesting town with lots of Cabarets, serving that good Japanese beer, lots of shopping areas, and some "on limits" restaurants. If you ate in one of the restaurants that didn't display an "On Limits" sign you could end up with a bad case of the "trots."(Diarrhea)

And believe it or not there were movie theaters showing American films, with Japanese sub titles. I remember seeing the movie Flying Tigers, with John Wayne, which as I recall did not show the Japanese in a very good light. I was amazed at that.

I was shopping for a China set for Flo and I wanted it to have Gold trim. As it turned out the Gold, at that point in time, was closely controlled and I couldn't get the China with Gold trim. I did buy Flo a very nice Silk Kimono, a beautiful Japanese doll, and a small hand made Japanese House, an elegant piece of hand work. She still has those items.

Speaking of the Japanese beer, which was served in one liter bottles, by the time you finished one of these beers your head would be aching and your bladder would be quite full. To relieve ones self you had to go outside and hunt down the local public toilet or "Benjo." The toilets in Japan are all unisex and you never can tell whom you will find in there. The first time I visited one I was standing at the urinal with some of my buddies when a pretty young Japanese girl entered looking for an open stall to relieve herself. Again we hooted and hollered at her and she looked at us like we were out of our minds! I guess we were, a little.

Toward the end of our tour in Japan I, and four other guys, took a train and went on R&R (Rest and Recuperation) to a resort on the western coast of Kyushu, at Karatsu. It was a beautiful place, right on the

DOWNTOWN FUKUOKA

CAMOFLAGED OIL TANKS -
THE STRIP - ITAZUKE

ME, TOM MENNELLA, CHUCK HALL - FUKUOKA

beach, and we were there probably for five or six days before returning to Itazuke. While we were there we took a boat tour of the local islands and Japanese shrines that were located on some of them. We had a very restful time.

When we returned, the squadron was about to pack up and move to Korea. So long to Itazuke and Japan, for the time being.

R & R (Rest & Recuperation) Hotel - Southern Coast of Kyushu

ME, PITTARD, MERWELLA
STILL ON R&R

On Tour - R&R

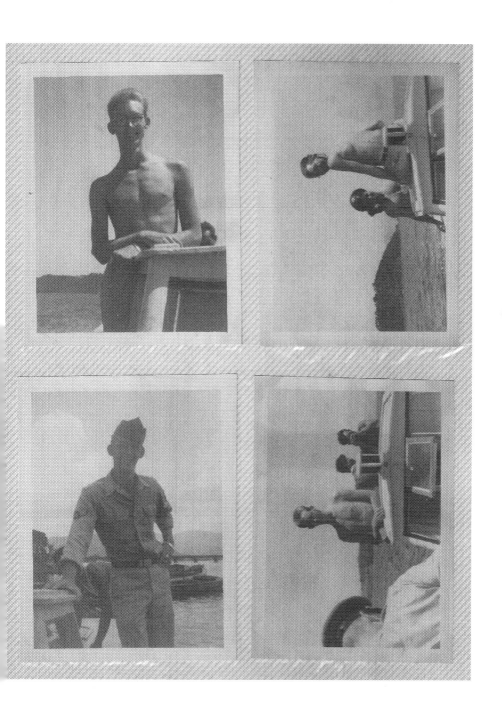

RICE PADDYS
TOP TO BOTTOM

GOODBYE
ITAZUKE

JAPANESE SHRINE

Chapter 8

THE 154ᵀᴴ F/B SQDN. AT K2, TAEGU, KOREA

IN AN OVERALL sense our "quality of life" took a definite turn for the worse when we moved from Japan to Korea. We went from living in fairly nice barracks to cold and drafty winterized tents that had seen better days. We did have electricity, two one-hundred watt bulbs hanging from their cords from the ridge pole.

Our toilet facilities went from normal to practically nothing. Our latrine consisted of a raised wooden platform that enclosed four cut off fifty-five gallon drums back to back, thus a "four holer," and was enclosed by a screened in structure with a door and roof over it. The screening minimized the flies to something less than a swarm while it allowed enough airflow so that one did not asphyxiate while attending to "nature's call." Also, nature's call did not necessarily wait for nice weather! In the dead of winter, and it really got bitterly cold in Korea, going potty in our "air conditioned" four holer was not something for the "faint of heart."

The toilet paper we used was newspapers (If you think that's funny try it sometime!), The Stars & Stripes, that had been well read. It's amazing what you can put up with when you are young.

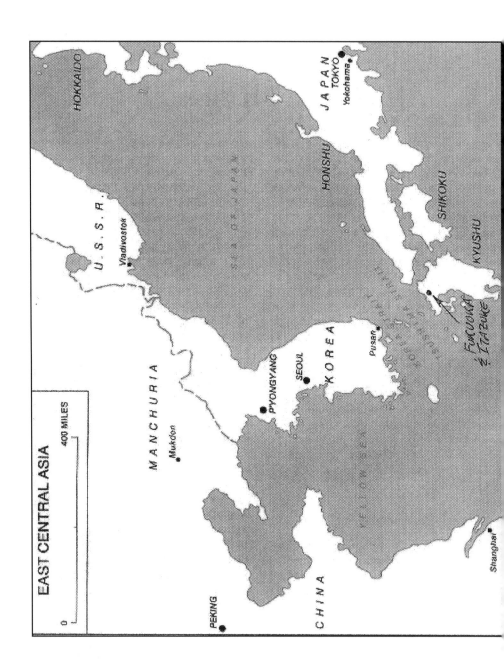

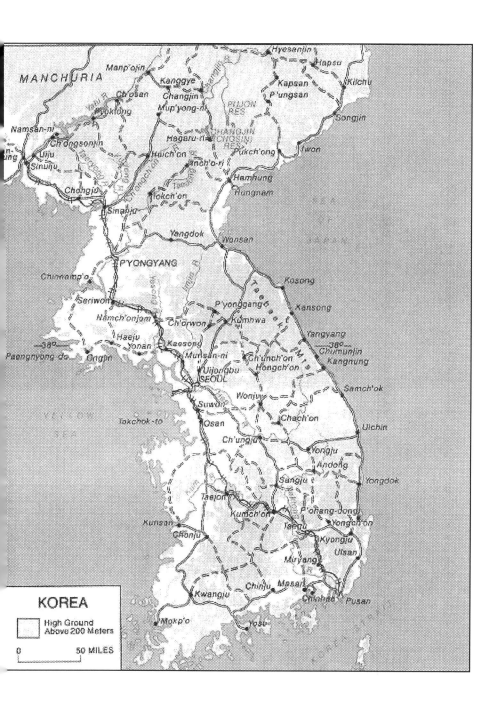

KOREA

High Ground
Above 200 Meters

0   50 MILES

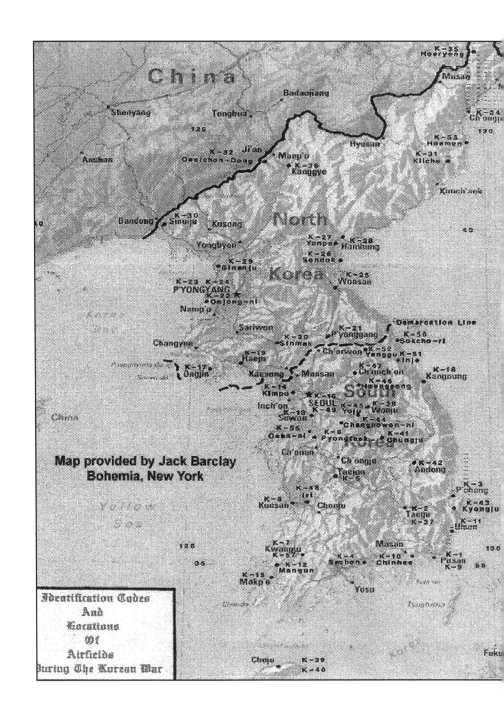

Map provided by Jack Barclay
Bohemia, New York

Identification Codes
And
Locations
Of
Airfields
During The Korean War

- 110 -

K2, Late '50 or Early '51

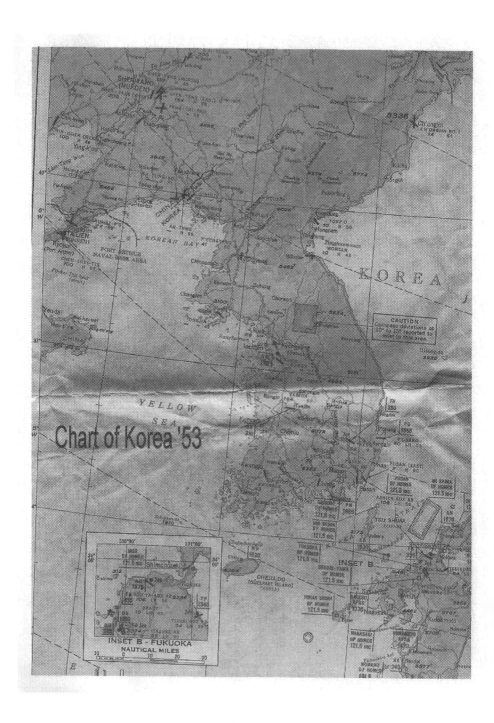

Chart of Korea '53

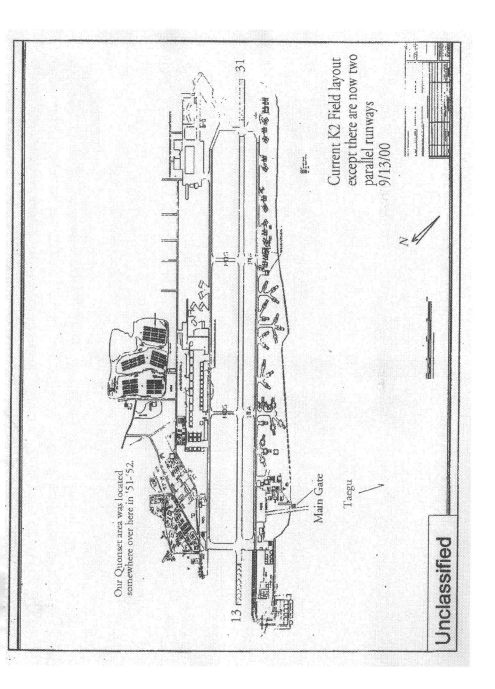

Our Quonset area was located somewhere over here in '51-'52.

Main Gate

Taegu

13

31

Current K2 Field layout except there are now two parallel runways
9/13/00

N

The shower we had was really a joke. It was located in a "Gunite" building, which in itself was not bad; however, the plumbing arrangement was a real mess. There was a small boiler to heat the water but somewhere in the bowels of this "plumber's nightmare" was a problem. As I recall, invariably in the middle of a shower when one was all soaped up, the warm water would come to an abrupt halt followed by nothing but cold, and I mean COLD, water! The Korean houseboy that tended the facility would be cursing in Korean while beating on the pipes with a club in order to free the vapor lock, all to no avail. Thus we minimized the showers taken and turned to washing in our tents using water heated in our helmets on the pot bellied stove. This is fondly called a "whores bath." We pretty much all stunk. Even with this situation we lived like Kings in comparison to the "foot soldiers" up on the front line.

One thing that did improve, again, was the mess hall. This also was in a Gunite building, which in it self was not impressive. But these cooks were the best I had ever come across in the service. They must have gone to Cooks and Bakers School, for real, because they really knew their stuff in my estimation. EVERY morning for breakfast we had eggs cooked to order on the griddle any way you wanted them, sunny side up, over easy, scrambled, you name it and the cook did it. Really first class! The rest of the meals were equally as good. Here we no longer had the luxury of trays to eat off of, we used our mess kits (which we fondly called s—t skillets) and canteen cups. On holidays our mess kits were over flowing with good food. If nothing else we ate well!

At K2 our armament area on the flight line initially consisted of a couple of large tents. In Korea we no longer had the luxury of indigenous labor as we did in Japan. When the machine guns needed cleaning, which they did most of the time, we did it. We also had longer workdays since we were located much closer to the targets in North Korea and thus flew more missions. Much of the time anyone spends in the service, no matter

OUR TENT AREA ON LEFT

MAIN STREET, K2 TAEGU, KOREA

RESULT OF COLLAPSED NOSE GEAR

"HI COOKIE" "KING SAO BAR"

MINER'S SPOT WHERE RUSTLESS FIVE FINALLY CRASHED

K2 FLIGHT LINE

HOME SWEET HOME

ME INSERTING A PROXIMITY FUZE

HELLO K2
TAEGU KOREA

TOM MENNELLA
FROM NEW YORK

OUR ARMAMENT TENTS
ON THE FLIGHT LINE - K2

ARMAMENT TENT
K2 FLT LINE SEPT 51

THIS MSGT WAS QUITE A CHARACTER

THE 154TH AIRCRAFT PARKED ON
THE PSP TAXIWAY (PERFORATED
STEEL PLANKING)

GUN CAMERA PORT

LOADING 500# BOMBS - IRAK

THIS ONE CRASHED & IS BEING STRIPPED OF USEFUL PARTS

500 POUND BOMB READY FOR FUZING

AIRCRAFT MAINTENANCE AREA ENGINE OVERHAUL BELOW

what branch, they spend WAITING! That is the way we passed a lot of our time down on the flight line. It was either hustle like crazy to get the aircraft loaded with bombs and rockets, or whatever the mission called for, or sit around and wait. Needless to say there was a lot of card playing.

When the planes returned from a mission we had to get the six .50 cal machine guns out of the aircraft, cleaned, and back into the planes and the ammo reloaded to be ready for the next mission. In between it was—wait!

Occasionally an aircraft would come back from a mission with its full load of ordnance still on board due to some malfunction. This was always fun time since all this stuff was quite live and had to be handled gingerly. The aircraft in this situation would stay out on the end of the runway and wait for us to come out and unload it. This didn't happen too often but when it did no one was too thrilled to handle this job.

The ordinance loads varied depending on the target for that day. The bombs came in various sizes, 260-pound fragmentation type, (which were anti-personnel), and 500, 1000, or 2000 pound GP or General Purpose bombs. Each bomb had two receptacles in them. One in the nose and one in the tail of the bomb, for fuses. There were three types of fuses that we used, Contact (which detonated when it hit something, like the ground), a VT or Proximity fuse (which had a small radio transmitter in it to detonate it at a certain height above ground), and Time Delay fuses, (to detonate at some fixed time after the bomb hits the ground, three hours, six hours, 12 hours, 24 hours.) The time delay fuses had an arrangement in them such that once they were screwed into the bomb they could not be removed without detonating the bomb. This prevented the enemy from disarming the bomb if found before it went off. In most cases, when we removed the protective plug from the sockets, the threads were fouled with explosive material that had seeped in during storage. This had to be carefully cleaned out in order to not set off the bomb while screwing in the fuse. Could ruin your whole day!!

The fuses themselves were quite safe. In order to set off the bomb they had to be "armed" and this was accomplished by a small propeller either on the nose or tail of the fuse depending on whether it was a nose or tail fuse. This propeller had to spin a certain number of times before it armed and was kept from spinning, while on the aircraft, by inserting an arming wire into the fuses which led up to an "arming solenoid" on the bomb rack. The pilot could choose to drop his ordinance either "safe" or "armed" depending on the position of the arming switch in the cockpit. If "armed" the arming wires would stay with the aircraft and as the bomb dropped the little propellers would spin arming the fuses. If "safe" were chosen, the arming wires would go with the bomb and since the fuses would not arm, the bomb would not explode.

Then there was the "Napalm." This was really nasty stuff and when the order came through to load Napalm you knew that the mission was probably "close support" for the infantry fighting somewhere up north on the 38th parallel. It was delivered to us on the flight line in metal containers that were about 18 inches in diameter and 8 feet long. They were really crude affairs, just seam welded together along their length, with bomb lugs on the top. On one side was the filling port, which was plugged with a wooden cap and toward the back was a welded on clamp for a fuse. The napalm was mixed up out in our bomb dump and could be mixed to different consistencies, thick or thin. If it was thick, it would stick to anything it hit and would burn long and hot. If it was thin, the effect would be a very white hot flash. Not much fun to be on the receiving end in either case!

We would load two of these containers on each aircraft. Once they were up in place on the bomb rack we would put the fuses in place. These were not conventional fuses but were really just "Phosphorous Grenades"

"Honey" Wagon Parade

Flight Line Armament Tent

Our "Super" Tent

imp

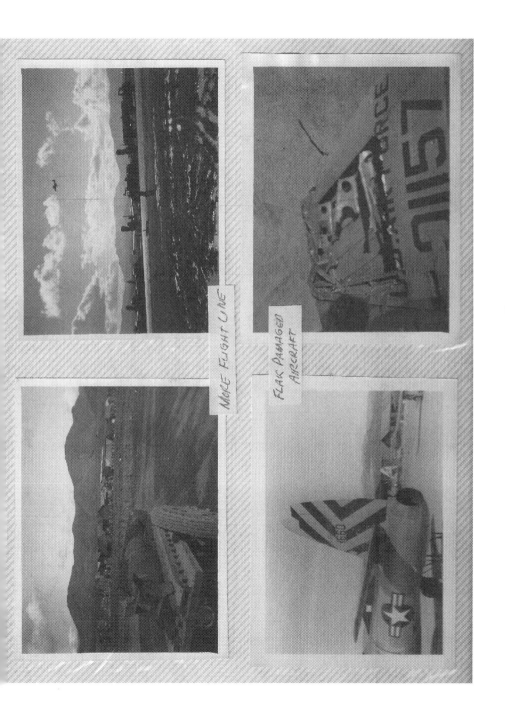

MORE FLIGHT LINE

FLAK DAMAGED
AIRCRAFT

ONE OF THE GUYS WITH A
SOCAL MACHINE GUN

SELF PORTRAITS
DRESSED FOR THE COLD

modified with an arming propeller. One went into the fill port and one fastened to the rear of the tank in the clamp. Again arming wires were put in place on the "fuses."

One day, after hanging the Napalm tanks on the aircraft, as I pulled the fill cap to insert the fuse the tank had been overfilled and the Napalm started to pour out. This stuff is much like snot and I had a heck of a time stopping it which I did by sticking in the grenade fuse. I ended up with a small puddle of it under the airplane, maybe two quarts or so that I had to dispose of. So I scooped it up by hand and put it in a bucket. Later after the aircraft had left on it's mission I took that bucket of Napalm and threw it on a rock behind the flight line and put a match to it. I couldn't believe how long and how hot that small amount of material burned. Nasty stuff, indeed!!

In mid October or so I was promoted to Flight chief of "C" flight, which consisted of four aircraft. Not bad for a guy that had made the s—t list a few months back. I guess they recognized that I knew my stuff. (If I don't blow my horn, who will?) Anyhow, things were running along pretty smoothly and I was getting along just fine with the guys in the flight working under me. The Lieutenant that was the officer in charge of our armament section thought I was doing a good job and told me he had put me in for Staff Sgt., that's three stripes and one "rocker." I was looking forward to that.

However, "other people" had different thoughts on that subject. In December our officer in charge transferred out and we got a new one. I was also relieved of duty as Flight Chief of "C" Flight and assigned to duty as "Ammunition Chief" for the squadron. In that capacity I had to requisition and prepare all of the .50 cal ammunition for our squadron of 16 aircraft and have all replacement ammunition cans ready at all times. That's four cans of 400 rounds each of ammo for each of the airplane's nose guns plus the 400 rounds that is needed for each of the two wing guns. That is a lot of ammo! In fact I had a tent full of it. This was all Armor Piercing Incendiary .50 caliber ammunition. I was also issued a 2 ½ ton GMC truck to haul this stuff around. It was a very good job. I had a crew of four airmen to help me plus help from the ROK (Republic of Korea) Airforce personnel.

Shortly after I got that job the promotion list was published, and guess what—I wasn't on it! The guy that took over as Flight Chief from me, naturally from Little Rock, got the extra stripe. I went in and asked the Lt. about the situation and told him that his predecessor had promised me another stripe. He said that when the list was reviewed, since he was new, he had asked the armament chief NCO (Sgt. Turner) for recommendations. I guess he still had it in for me. I only did one thing before I just let it go and that was to tell the kid that got the extra stripe that he should enjoy wearing MY stripe! He didn't say a word and just kind of gave me the "fish eye."

I have to tell you that this 6x6 truck I had was really a good vehicle. It had 5 speeds forward with one reverse and optional 6-wheel drive (really 10-wheel drive since it had four sets of duals on the rear). In 6-wheel drive I had the option of a high or low range. In low range I believe that vehicle would be able to push its way through a brick wall. Anyhow, that transmission was so smooth I could shift it up and down through the 5 gears without touching the clutch! I rarely used 1st gear since it was so low but if I wasn't using the clutch I would give the engine a little goose and pull it into low. The truck would jump a little and I would then accelerate. I would then push the gearshift into neutral, another little goose and shift into 2nd, and so on all the way into 5th. I would follow the same procedure on the way down through the gears. Never ground a gear or clicked a tooth, it was almost like an automatic transmission!

One day while hauling trash out to the dump for some reason I had to turn around. The road there was just one skinny lane with rice paddies on both sides. So I put it in 6 wheel drive low range and just chugged my way through those paddies until I was turned around and back on the road. The truck never faltered. Those rice paddies are quite deep, as I recall about 2 to 3 feet. That truck was a little smelly until I could get it hosed down.

It was kind of interesting out in the dump area, which was located right next to a small Korean village. Or was the village located next to the dump? Probably the latter since we Americans are noted for throwing away some really good "stuff." When we came out with a load of trash the whole village would turn out to salvage all the useful materials. More than half the people out there were the Korean women and quite a few of them were carrying small "papooses" on their backs. A lot of these little babies were sporting blond hair and that could only mean one thing, the GI's had been visiting. These kids were invariably ostracized from Korean society since they were "half breeds." That was a real tragedy.

When I was getting close to the end of my tour I was told to get my replacement checked out in the truck before he took his driving test. This guy apparently had never driven a stick shift in his life and I had a real struggle teaching him how. I took him out into the middle of the airfield, the wide-open spaces, where he could concentrate on shifting gears and didn't have to mind the road. He still couldn't get it. After a few trips up and down the field I figured I was making him nervous so I got out and told him to take it for a spin solo. By the time he returned he had taken two gears out of it!! I don't think he ever did get the knack of using a clutch. When I took the truck into the motor pool to get it repaired I really took a lot of "flak". They had it repaired in a few days.

One morning, a mission to North Korea was getting underway and was to be led by the Wing Commander Col. Prendergast. When the signal came for the pilots to "start engines" I guess the Col. got too anxious on the throttle and flooded the engine with fuel before it was up to RPM.

You have to remember these aircraft and jet engines were from the late 1940's era and not as sophisticated as the engines of today. When starting these engines the pilot had to watch the tachometer and make sure it was up to the proper RPM before cracking the throttle. If he came in with the throttle too soon the engine would flood with fuel, the fire would go out and raw fuel would pour out of the tail pipe.

Then before attempting restart the pilot was supposed to wait about 10 minutes for the engine to drain of excess fuel. If he didn't he could get a "hot start" which meant the fuel puddled in the tail pipe would ignite and the tail pipe would overheat and be damaged. That is exactly what happened with the Col. He only waited about 5 minutes and when he did start, flame shot out of the tail pipe about 15 feet long. Spectacular but not good for the engine!

As it was, the rest of the squadron was already airborne and gone when he started to taxi out for take off. Instead of aborting the mission, as he should have, he chose to go and try to catch up. Unfortunately that was the last we saw of the Col. I don't know if anyone knows exactly what happened to him but I think one or two pilots saw him standing in a riverbed, up north, close to the Yellow sea, waving.

I believe it was sometime in December of 1951 when we bade adieu to our faithful tents and moved into our new Quonset Huts. By comparison this was like moving up to the Hilton Hotel. They were warm and dry and comfortable. It was like living in a barracks again. I appreciated it. Even the latrine was great! Warm water was usually plentiful and the "john" (toilet) was quite an improvement. This was the equivalent of a 15 holer running down the one side of the hut with an automatic flusher to wash the waste away. Hog heaven! No more swarms of flies and stink and no more bathing out of my helmet. Even when the water was cold, which was often, it was great.

A very junior US Navy Lt. (jg) Walter M. Schirra, Jr., serving on exchange duty with the 154th FBS, gets strapped into the cockpit of an F-84E Thunderjet at Taegu for a mission over North Korea, with help from Sergeant Harrison, crew chief of the aircraft. Schirra later became one of the original "Mercury Seven" astronauts, and the only astronaut to fly in space in all three major American programs— Mercury, Gemini, and Apollo. *Robert L. Bell.*

K-2, Taegu, Korea. '51-'52

This F-84, from the 111th FBS, sustained damage over N. Korea. A 20mm round came in through the engine intake and exploded on the upper edge of the front armor plate. It blew out the right front plexi windscreen and blinded the pilot who was able to fly back to K-2 and land!

COCKPIT, ME & CREWCHIEF
OF TRIPLE 3

154TH SQUADRON EMBLEM

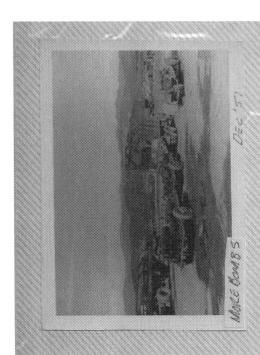

DEC '51

MORE BOMBS

ROK AIRMEN

TWO STARS
MEANS 2 MIGS
SHOT DOWN

DON MCDONALD ON LEFT

NEW 154TH AIRMAN QUT BAAR

I BUILT THIS CHART WITH WOOD SO THAT IT COULD BE REMOVED

JP4 FUELED POT BELLIED STOVE

READY FOR A MISSION

JUST OFF THE GROUND & GEAR UP

THE RED CROSS "MUD WAGON" TIME FOR FRESH COFFEE & DONUTS

STARTING ENGINES

KICKING UP DUST
OR WATER PLUME

THE 154TH ON THEIR WAY
TO NORTH KOREA - DEC '51

HERE'S A KISS
FROM FLO
TO JOE!

JOE STALIN

JOHN PIERCE - NOSE GUN —
AMMO CANS ON LEFT

Tom Mennella

Don McDonald

Steve Polkabla

Mennella &
Friend

NEW QUONSET HUT LIVING
AREA - FINALLY OUT OF TENTS

AMMUNITION
STORAGE CAVE

HOME SWEET HOME, 1941

SAM BASS WITH SHINER
& MISSING TOOTH

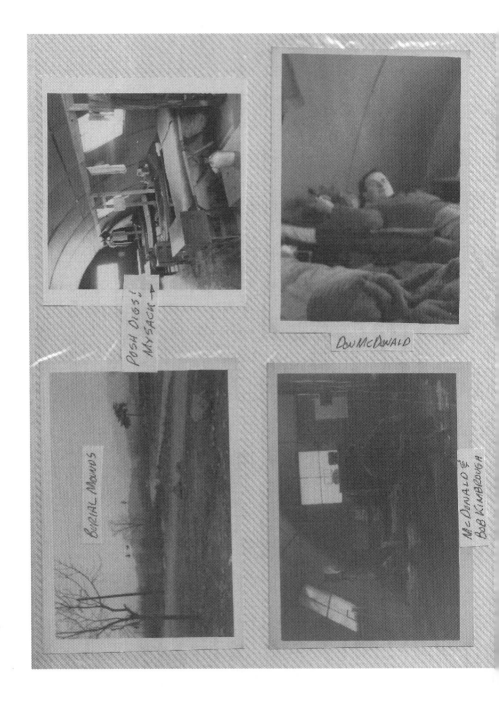

POSH DIGS!
MYSACK →

DON McDONALD

BURIAL MOUNDS

McDONALD &
BOB KIMBROUGH

STEVE POLKABLA

WHO'S MAD?

STEVE & FRIEND

WINTER LINE
GEAR

ME WITH PIPE -
AMMO TENT BEHIND

ME & STEVE

THIS GUY WAS LUCKY TO GET BACK! EITHER THE TURBINE BLEW OR HIT BY FLAK.

JOHN ACREE & ME

AN F-86 THAT WANDERED INTO K2

Next to the latrine were a couple of gigantic covered cesspools. About once every two weeks or so the local "honey dumpers" would be invited in to empty these pits. These Korean men, usually 6 or 8 per latrine, would come in with their horse drawn "honey wagons" and proceed to empty our cesspools, by hand, with long handled dippers. These wagons were about the size of a small trailer. ALL of this waste material would subsequently be watered down, sold to the local farmers, and used to fertilize the local crops, be it rice, vegetables or whatever. These were usually pretty smelly operations and it was wise to keep clear of the latrine area during these times. To illustrate how short these people were on any kind of fertilizer, the horses had burlap bags fastened under their tails to catch any manure that the horses dropped while hauling the wagons. Nothing went to waste!!

Again I found I was having a problem with one of my teeth. I went on sick call and made an appointment with the dentist. This was really a treat. When I got in to see him he took a look in my mouth and said he recognized that a graduate of North Western University had done my dental work, which was true. Quite perceptive! He had to do a little drilling. This was accomplished by having his assistant mount what appeared to be a stationary bicycle just behind the dental chair. He was the power for the drill! This meant the drill speed was relatively slow, no heat build up, and no pain. I can truthfully say this was one of the few times I enjoyed a visit to the dentist.

In December of 1951 I was due for some R&R (rest and recuperation) so one of my armament mates (Jim Roman who was also from Cleveland, OH) and I packed our gear, donned our dress blues and headed for Tokyo. We took a shuttle flight out of K2 and ended up at Tachikawa AFB, just outside of Tokyo. We arrived at night and took the RT (railway transit) into town. It had recently snowed and was quite cold. When we got into the train station in downtown Tokyo we were swarmed by Japanese men hustling everything from hotel rooms to taxi rides and everything in

READY FOR R&R IN TOKYO 2-52

ERNIE PYLE THEATRE IN TOKYO - SAW "THE RED SHOES"

STOCKADE AT K2 (JAIL)

JIM ROMANS & ME IN TOKYO AIR MEN'S CLUB

JAPANESE CEMETERY

BACK FROM R & R

DIA ICHI BLDG IN TOKYO
McARTHUR'S HEADQUARTERS

MOAT AROUND EMPEROR'S
PALACE IN TOKYO

ARMAMENT SHACK ON THE
FLIGHT LINE AT K2 - ME & JIM

ME-SMOKING PIPE, JIM RANDS, PETE STULL

ME IN CENTER

between. We picked one guy and said we wanted a nice Japanese hotel and he immediately took us to a taxi, put us in the back seat and, shouted something to the driver. We were off, to where we didn't have a clue!!

By the way, most of the taxis I saw were old 1934 Fords that had been modified by installing a small diesel engine in them. The way they were driven was unique. The driver would get the vehicle going about 50 miles an hour and then shift into neutral, kill the engine, and coast. I really doubt if this did anything to increase their mileage, but I guess they thought so and that's what counts. These Japanese drivers I think were all certifiably crazy! Our driver would race at a blind intersection and never make a motion like he was going to stop, and he never did. Jim and I could only brace ourselves in the back seat and hope for the best. When we would fly through the intersections, miraculously there would be no traffic! I don't understand it but we survived.

We seemed to be getting further and further off the main streets and Jim and I started to look at one another wondering what was in store for us. We could have easily ended up dead and no one would have been the wiser.

Anyhow, before long we were going down this dark alley and appearing out of the darkness was the well-lit front of what turned out to be a very new and quaint Japanese hotel. The place even smelled new! We were instructed to remove our shoes outside at the door (a very smart Japanese custom) and were ushered inside. We arranged for our room, which was nicely furnished with Futons, for sleeping, and a Hibachi (charcoal burner) to keep the room warm. This place was really neat and even had a small Japanese garden behind it, which in itself was very beautiful.

During the day we did a lot of sight seeing, such as the outside of the Emperor's palace, and in the evenings we headed for the Tokyo Airman's Club. This club, in my estimation, had to be the equivalent of any of our better nightclubs in the "states". There must have been at least three dining rooms, all very cozy and serving excellent meals at very low prices. There also must have been three bars and one room had a band and a large dance floor surrounded by tables. When the band wasn't playing they had shows put on which were very good! And the drinks were not only good, and made with top shelf liquor, but cost the equivalent of $.10 apiece! We gave the waiter a $2 tip and we couldn't put the drinks away fast enough. He was back every two minutes asking if we needed another drink! Needless to say we were feeling no pain when we left that place. Jim and I spent a lot of time in that club.

After about 5 days we headed back to Tachikawa to catch our plane back to K2. Some of the guys took leave time and headed for such exotic places like Singapore and Hong Kong. Why I didn't do that I have no idea. One thing I should have done while we were at Itazuke was to go to Hiroshima. It was not that far away but I guess I had other things on my mind.

Back at K2 it was back to the old grind. The weather in Korea was usually extreme. When it was hot in the summer it was HOT and in the winter it was COLD! Luckily we had plenty of foul weather gear so we rarely felt it while working on the aircraft.

In the winter, with the air nice and dense, the F84's had no trouble getting off the runway with their ordnance loads. In hot weather the story was quite different and bomb loads had to be limited and in most cases JATO (actually rocket or jet assisted take off) bottles had to be hung on the aircraft to assist them in getting airborne.

Sometimes the airplanes wouldn't get airborne and would go sliding off the end of our 10,000 foot runway, right into the farmers rice paddy tearing the airplane and the paddy all to hell! In most cases the pilots of these birds would be unhurt, maybe a little smelly but unhurt. I think the

A SNOWY DAY AT K2 - FEB '52

Me & ROK AIR FORCE GUYS

A T-33

farmer that owned that rice paddy loved to see us tear it up since he got paid, probably handsomely, every time it happened.

Sometime in December we got word that a USO troupe would be coming to the base to entertain us. The group that came included Piper Laurie, a Hollywood starlet at that time, and Johnny Grant, a prominent Los Angeles disc jockey. (Johnny is currently the honorary mayor of LA and quite a celebrity.) There were a few other folks but I don't remember who they were. I do remember the day they put on the, show, which was a good one, and as I recall the troops enjoyed and appreciated it. I also recall that the officers got all of the good front row seats. I didn't begrudge the pilots those seats but some of the other officers shouldn't have had that luxury.

The one and only time I went into Taegu was to go to Mass on Christmas Eve 1951. We were loaded into 6x6s and driven into Taegu. When we got into town we were taken to a large Catholic Cathedral where we were all taken inside. As I remember the front half of the church was taken up by Koreans and we, the GIs, filled the back half. It was very large and ornate and it seemed to me quite smoky at the time. One other guy that I correspond with remembers it as the only time he went to church where some of the people had guns. I don't remember that. There were two pulpits, one for the front half of the church and one for the back half. We did get a sermon in English.

Going into Taegu I guess had it's risks, even in the daytime. Vehicles taken into town were to be parked in a special compound guarded by MPs. I heard stories about guys taking Jeeps or trucks into town and not adhering to this rule. When they returned, after leaving their vehicles for a time, they found them up on blocks with all the wheels missing! If they were lucky shortly they were offered a set of wheels, probably from the Koreans that had stolen them, for their vehicle at an exorbitant price. Did they have a choice? It was buy or face court marshal.

USO CHRISTMAS SHOW WITH PIPER LAURIE & JOHNNIE GRANT MAYOR OF LA

OUR LONELY CHRISTMAS TREE 1951

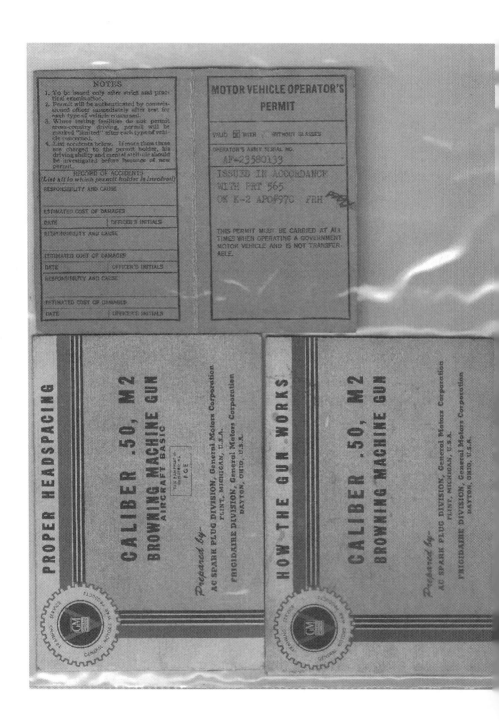

DATE OF ISSUE

22 January 1952   EXPIRES 22 Jan 53

OPERATOR'S SIGNATURE

Donald J. Paul.

I CERTIFY THAT DONALD J. PAUL   SGT
                        (NAME AND GRADE)

HAS DEMONSTRATED PROFICIENCY IN DRIVING *(change 4, par. 24, AR 850-15)* THE TYPES OF VEHICLES LISTED BELOW AS PER SIGNED AUTHENTICATION.

TYPE VEHICLE	AUTHENTICATION *(Signed by a commissioned officer)*
CAR, HALFTRACK	
CAR, PASSENGER	
MOTORCYCLE	
TANK, HEAVY	
TANK, LIGHT	
TANK, MEDIUM	
TRACTOR	
TRUCK-TRACTOR *(semitrailer)*	
TRUCKS, CARGO, ¾-¾-TON FRH	FRH
TRUCKS, CARGO, 1½-2½-TON FRH	FRH
TRUCKS, CARGO, 4-TON AND LARGER	
TRUCKS, AMPHIBIAN *(all)*	
VEHICLE, WHEELED, COMBAT	
SPECIAL	

DA AGO FORM 9-74   REPLACES WD AGO FORM 9-74, 17 JUN 44,
   1 AUG 48   WHICH MAY BE USED.

ME & GUYS AT
AMMO TENT

JATO BOTTLE

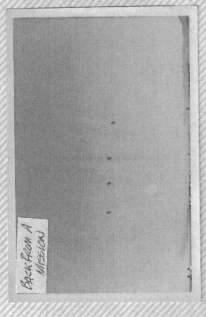

BACK FROM A
MISSION

ME & MY AMMO
TRUCK

HILLS TO THE WEST

ME & JIM ROMAN FUSING 5 IN
ROCKET-NAPALM CANNISTER
ON BOMB RACK

NO AFTERBURNER!

LOADING THE WING GUNS WITH
50 CAL AMMO

HEADING FOR JAPAN - AUX.
FUEL TANKS ON BOMB RACKS

HEADING FOR N. KOREA WITH
TWO 500 LB BOMBS - USING
JATO FOR HOT WEATHER TAKEOFF

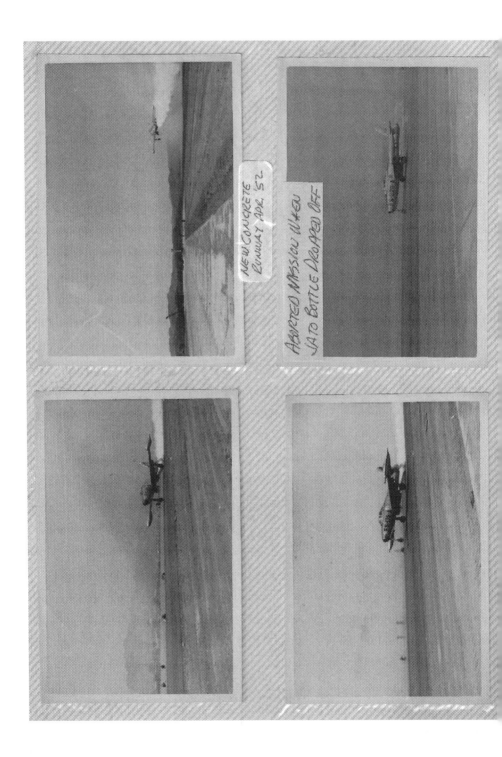

NEW CONCRETE RUNWAY APR. 52.

ABORTED MISSION WHEN JATO BOTTLE DROPPED OFF

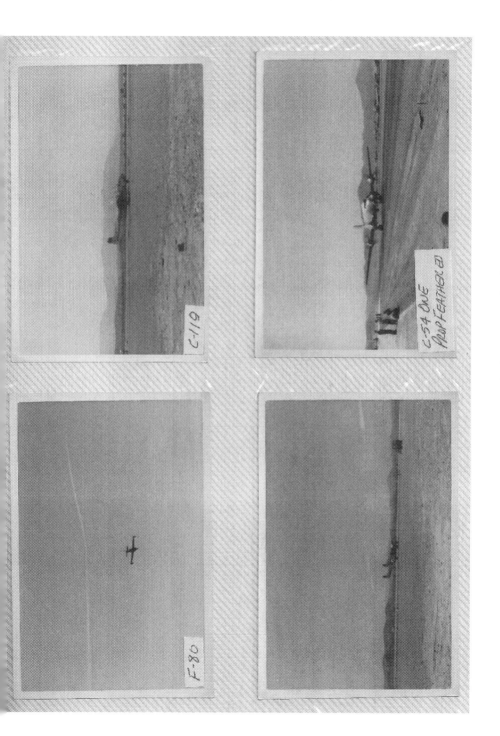

C-119

C-54 ONE
PROP FEATHERED

F-80

Jim Rohan

CHUCK HALL

ROK AIRMAN

LOTTSA BOMBS

ALAMO TENT

SHORTY

HONEY WAGON

RUSSIAN T-34 TANK IN RIVER
BED NORTH PERIMETER K-2

THE ARMAMENT
"GANG"

KOREAN LADIES
DOING LAUNDRY

AFTERBURNER ON F94

RADAR AT K2

B-26 INVADER

F-94

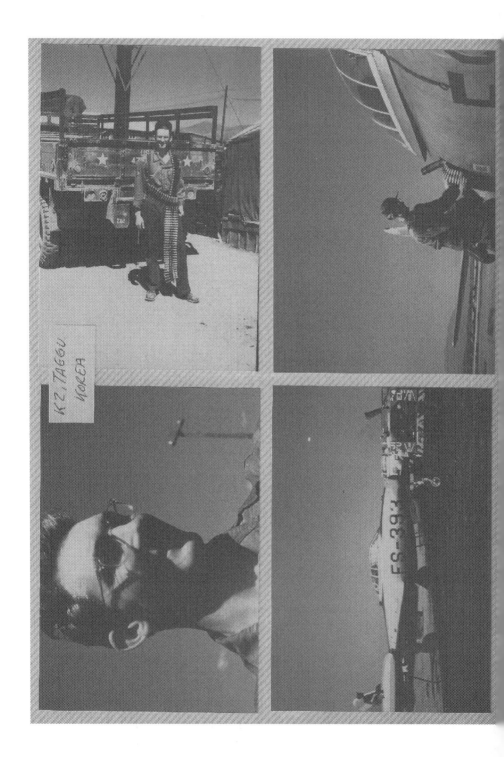

K2, TAGU
KOREA

JATO BOTTLE

BURNED OUT RUSSIAN T34
TANK IN DRY RIVERBED
JUST NORTH OF K2

KOREAN VILLAGE

BOB KIMBROUGH
& JIM ROMAN

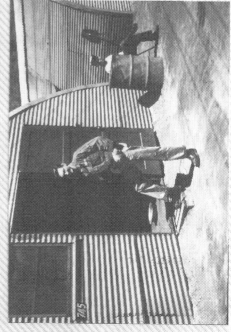

My understanding is that the Black Market operated openly in and around Taegu and probably in all of Korea, south of the battle lines, for that matter. I always wondered why they just didn't shut it down and arrest all of the people involved. The story I got was if that were to happen the Korean economy would collapse, so they just left it alone. Who's to know?

I think it was sometime in early 1952, maybe March or so, while the peace talks were going on and our ground forces were caught in the "meat grinder" up on the 38th Parallel, that the Red Cross decided to pack their operation up and leave K2. They were to move up closer to the front where the fighting was going on. It turned out to be a sad day for us troops. Air Force Special Services people replaced them. No more "Mud Wagon" was coming down the line serving fresh donuts and hot coffee, FOR FREE! Now we had to go to their facility and BUY the stuff! What a blow! Things were never the same. The Red Cross facility, that was open 24 hours a day, was turned into the K2 Passenger Terminal. What a miserable place that turned out to be. I guess all good things must come to an end.

Then one day it happened, probably sometime in April!! I was called to headquarters and was given a set of orders, MY ORDERS TO GO HOME FOR DISCHARGE!! Oh happy day! I quickly went back to the barracks and sat down and penned a letter to Flo and also one to my folks informing them of the news. She said that that was the best letter she ever received. I know it was one of the happiest ones I ever wrote.

I immediately hung up a calendar and started to "X" off the days. I couldn't believe how the days started to drag! I guess it's like staring at your watch, the time really goes by sooooo slowly.

Finally the day arrived and I was more than ready to go. We hauled all our earthly possessions over to the "K2 Air Terminal" (what a dump) and

SPECIAL ORDERS)   4 May 1952
NUMBER   75)   E X T R A C T

14. Fol named USAF amn are reld fr asgmt & dy orgns indicated & rsgd to
xxx Pers Proc Sq FEAMCOM Area "B" APO 959 for further trans to ZI under shipmt
no MAY-24 for purpose of rels fr EAD UP AFL 39-12. FEAF May Returnee. Amn WP
o/a 17 May 52 fr Det 1, 136th Ftr Bmr Wg APO 929 to Higashi Fuchu Japan so as
to arr not earlier than 0001 hrs and NLT 1500 hrs 19 May 52. PCS PCA TDN TBMAA
T96A4. Nec rail and/or bus trans auth. 5723500 248-341 P533(5) -02-03-05-07
S99-999 AUTH: AFR 35-59 & 5th AF Msg FRA 249 dtd 28 Apr 52. EDCSA 25 May 52.

M SGT DAVID L BAKER AF 38602347 (Sv Cat E) (W) (Comp ANG) (PAFSC 90670) (Ship
AFSC 90670) (DOS 25 Jun 52) (Home address: 2409 Louisiana St, Little Rock Ark)
136th Med Gp APO 970.

M SGT SAMUEL K MORGAN AF 25430077 (Sv Cat E) (W) (Comp ANG) (PAFSC 43170)
(Ship AFSC 43170) (DOS 9 Jul 52) (Home address: 1715 Chandler St, N Little
Rock Ark) Hq 136 Ftr Bmr Gp APO 970.

T SGT EDWARD M CHRISP JR AF 38290824 (Sv Cat E) (W) (Comp ANG) (PAFSC 32270)
(Ship AFSC 32270) (DOS 10 Sep 52) (Home address: 2604 E 6th St, Little Rock Ark)
154 Ftr Bmr Sq 136 Ftr Bmr Gp presently atchd 136 Maint Sq 136 M & S Gp APO 970.

T SGT ABELARDO E DELGADO AF 36952761 (Sv Cat E) (W) (Comp ANG) (PAFSC 43170H)
(Ship AFSC 43170H)(DOS 9 Jul 52) (Home address: 131 Cavalier Ave, San Antonio
Tex) 182d Ftr Bmr Sq 136th Ftr Bmr Gp APO 970.

T SGT AUGUSTINE PAZ JR AF 20801132 (Sv Cat E) (W) (Comp ANG) (PAFSC 30170)
(Ship AFSC 30170)(DOS 9 Jul 52) (Home address: 2815 Perez St, San Antonio Tex)
182d Ftr Bmr Sq, 136th Ftr Bmr Gp APO 970.

S SGT MONTGOMERY L BELL AF 25430274 (Sv Cat E) (W) (Comp ANG) (PAFSC 43153)
(Ship AFSC 43153)(DOS 23 Jun 52) (Home address: 119 McCullogh St, San Antonio
Tex) 136th Maint Sq 136th M & S Gp APO 970.

S SGT JOHN A DILLARD AF 38649104 (Sv Cat E) (W) (Comp ANG) (PAFSC 46250)
(Ship AFSC 46250) (DOS 9 Jul 52) (Home address: 8328 Garland Ave, Houston
Tex) 182d Ftr Bmr Sq 136th Ftr Bmr Gp APO 970.

S SGT JOHN D HESSON AF 25430364 (Sv Cat E) (W) (Comp ANG) (PAFSC 90150)
(Ship AFSC 90150) (DOS 25 Jun 52) (Home address: 209 Morgan St, Phoenixville
Pa) 136th Med Gp APO 970.

S SGT BRUCE H SIMPSON AF 18290733 (Sv Cat E) (W) (Comp ANG) (PAFSC 90650)
(Ship AFSC 90650) (DOS 25 Jun 52) (Home address: 2300 Bragg St, Little Rock
Ark) 136th Med Gp APO 970.

HEADQUARTERS, 136TH FIGHTER BOMBER WING, APO 970   4 May 1952
SO 75 PAR 10 CONT'D

A/3C ERNEST F WISE AF 18345469 (Sv Cat E) (W) (Comp ANG) (PAFSC 43170H)
(Ship AFSC 43170H)(DOS 9 Jul 52) (Home address: 134 Caldwell St, San Antonio
Tex) 182d Ftr Bmr Sq 136th Ftr Bmr Gp APO 970.

A/1C DONALD L HESTIR AF 57430532 (Sv Cat E) (W) (Comp ANG) (PAFSC 43151H)
(Ship AFSC 43151H) (DOS 8 Jul 53) (Home address: Lonoke Ark) 154th Ftr Bmr
Sq Ftr Bmr Gp APO 970.

A/2C PERRY R HOOD AF 25994143 (Sv Cat E) (W) (Comp ANG) (PAFSC 95150) (Ship
AFSC 95150) (DOS 9 Jul 52) (Home address: Rt 2, Bx 514, Irving Tex) 136th
Instl Sq 136th Air Base Gp APO 970.

A/1C DONALD J PAUL AF 23560133 (Sv Cat E) (Comp ANG) (W) (PAFSC 46250) (Ship
AFSC 46250) (DOS 18 Sep 53) (Home address: 4221 W 50th St, Cleveland Ohio)
154th Ftr Bmr Sq 136th Ftr Bmr Gp APO 970.

A/1C FRED L PIURDOLLA AF 25897164 (Sv Cat E) (W) (Comp ANG) (PAFSC 43133)
(Ship AFSC 43133) (DOS 9 Jul 52) (Home address: Bx 26, LaVernia Tex) 182d
Ftr Bmr Sq 136th Ftr Bmr Gp APO 970.

A/1C JUAN D SMITH AF 25430238 (Sv Cat E) (W) (Comp ANG) (PAFSC 64131) (Ship
AFSC 64131) (DOS 13 Jul 53) (Home address: 2317 Summitt, Little Rock Ark)
111th Ftr Bmr Sq 136th Ftr Bmr Gp APO 970.

A/3C JOCOB G ESCOBEDO AF 26005047 (Sv Cat E) (W) (Comp ANG) (PAFSC 46230)
(Ship AFSC 46230)(DOS 9 Jul 52) (Home address: 305½ N San Saba, San Antonio
Tex) 182d Ftr Bmr Sq 136th Ftr Bmr Gp APO 970.

M SGT DOUGLAS L NIKLE AF 18154840 (Sv Cat E) (W) (Comp ANG) (PAFSC 43171H)
(Ship AFSC 43171H)(DOS 9 Jul 52) (Home address: 234 Dulling St, San Antonio
Tex) 136th Maint Sq 136th M & S Gp atch fr 182d Ftr Bmr Sq 136 Ftr Bmr Gp
APO 970.

          BY ORDER OF COLONEL BUCK:

OFFICIAL: M.R. SERVISS
                                   Capt., USAF
                                   Adjutant

M.R. SERVISS
Capt., USAF
Adjutant

DISTRIBUTION:
  "Z" Plus
  Ea Ann - 25
  Ea Orgn 2 Per Indiv
  Wg Comptroller - 4

HERE ARE THE ORDERS SENDING ME HOME!

waited for our air transportation. A C-47 "Gooney Bird" showed up and this was to take us to Itazuke, our previous base, for preliminary processing prior to going up to Tachikawa. While waiting I noticed that one of my fellow "rotatees" was packing some really nice camera equipment. He had a 16MM Bolex movie camera and a 35MM Nikon SLR camera, both items brand new and very expensive! This guy was from the 154th and was an assistant crew chief on one of our F-84s. Another of the guys going back was the crew chief on the same airplane. I asked him where he got all the money for these items and initially he was hesitant to answer. He cast a glance at his crew chief who nodded his assent to answering my question. At this point he related this story.

One evening he and his crew chief were in Taegu, just wandering around, when a Korean man stopped them and asked if they ever got back to Japan. They said they did and why was he asking. The man produced a small cubical can about 2 inches on a side decorated in oriental markings and said it was "soup seasoning." The two GIs said "Yeah, right." The man urged them to take the can and on their next visit to Japan and check it out. He also said he would pay them top dollar and buy all that they could deliver to him. On their next run back to Itazuke to service their airplane they went into Fukuoka and checked it out, and sure enough it was soup seasoning! So they bought $35 worth, which was quite a bit of soup seasoning and took it back to K2 with them on board their flight. I don't know how much they got for this first delivery and I don't know how long they kept up this operation but they did say that in the end they had made $25,000!! Not a bad turnover for a $35 investment.

However, this was a "black market" operation and subjected these guys to possible court marshal and subsequent prison terms if prosecuted and found guilty of using government transportation. They split the money $15,000 for the chief and $10,000 for the assistant. A nice piece of change in the early '50s!!

LEAVING K2, KOREA FOR ITAZUKE, JAPAN BY C47

JAPANESE COUNTRYSIDE—ON TRAIN TO TOKYO AREA

We arrived at Itazuke the same day. As I recall I was billeted in the same barracks I was in when we left some nine months earlier. The first thing I did was strip off and jump in the shower!! I believe I stayed in that soothing hot shower at least an hour!! It must have taken that long to get that Korean grime off my body.

We stayed at Itazuke long enough to get our paperwork straightened out. We were then put aboard a rickety train which took us from Itazuke on up to Tachikawa AFB, which is close to Tokyo. This was an overnight trip and we had sleepers to bed down in at night. As I recall quite a bit of the countryside was still showing signs of devastation from all the bombing of Japan during WWII.

Chapter 9

THE 154ᵀᴴ F/B SQUADRON AT K2, TAEGU, KOREA INCIDENTS AT K2

ABOUT THE MIDDLE of September 1951 the 136th F/B wing started to pack up to move to a field in south Korea called K2 close to the city of Taegu. If you recall, when the North Koreans first started the hostilities in June of 1950, they pushed the allied forces down into a pocket in South Korea fondly called the "Pusan Perimeter." K2, Taegu was on the northern edge of that perimeter and was one of the holding points for the allied forces. Rumor had it that our P-51s were flying FIVE-MINUTE missions out of K2 and in some cases not even retracting their landing gear prior to dumping their ordinance on the approaching North Korean forces. That was their total air time before returning to K2 to reload! I am thankful that I was not there at that time to witness that spectacle.

Due to the bold planning of General MacArthur, and the guts of the US Marines, the landing at Inchon, in September of '50, took the wind out of the Northern Korean push south and the battle lines quickly moved toward the north. By the time we arrived at K2 the battle had surged all the way up to the Yalu River and the Chosin Reservoir, where the Chinese forces suddenly entered the war, and had come back down to the 38th

Parallel where the battle had stagnated. As I recall the peace talks started not too long after our arrival, which we all hoped, would bring a hasty end to this crazy business. Alas, it was not to be and the war dragged on. The following is a compilation of a lot of the incidents that happened on the way to and during the stay of the 154th F/B squadron at K2, Taegu, Korea.

This one happened when we moved from Itazuke, Japan to K2, Korea.

CRAZY PILOTS

We were shipped to K2, Korea in September '51. At Itazuke, Japan all the personnel and their gear were loaded into C-54s and flown over to K2. That in itself was an adventure!

When we were on board the aircraft the pilot started the engines and called for the chocks and tail strut to be removed. The C-54 had a tail strut that was pinned in place to keep the aircraft from banging it's tail down in high winds. Well, the loadmaster did a bum job of loading this bird because the ground crew couldn't remove the strut! The whole center aisle was loaded with equipment with the GI's sitting along the sides of the fuselage and in the rear, where some other guys and I were located. When they couldn't remove the strut the pilot motioned for some of us people in the rear of the aircraft to come forward to the cockpit, which we did. Good old weight and balance! As I recall they still couldn't remove the strut. So the pilot shoved the yoke to the firewall, stood on the brakes, and gunned the engines. That did the trick and the strut came out. We taxied all the way out to the runway with the pilot holding the yoke all the way forward, the engines roaring, and riding the brakes! The takeoff run was quite long and I recall when it came time to rotate for takeoff the pilot just barely moved the control column off the firewall and we were airborne! These military pilots sure have a lot of leeway when it comes to operating their aircraft. I guess he didn't want to take the time to unload and reshuffle the cargo. It turns out that was a very dangerous situation with the center of gravity that far aft.

Another time, at K2, I was out on the field watching the aircraft take off when another C-54 taxied into position for take off. I noticed he only had three engines running. The port inboard engine wasn't running and the prop was feathered. He began his takeoff run and about halfway down the strip he unfeathered the prop and fired it up! I guess the starter was out and he figured this was as good away as any to get that engine going.

A few days before they moved all the personnel and gear to Korea the pilots ferried all of our aircraft from the wing over to K2. The runway over at K2 was 10,000 feet long and made out of PSP (perforated steel planking). I guess our pilots had gotten used to landing on nice smooth concrete runways because we heard that most of them had blown their tires when they put down at K2.

When we got to K2 all the personnel and their gear were moved to a tent area on the Northeast corner of the field. We were back to living in 'winterized' squad tents with two pot bellied stoves for heat. As I recall there were 10 cots in each tent. Luckily the potbellies ran on either kerosene or JP-1 jet fuel. Outside the tent on one side there was a wooden cradle holding a 55-gallon drum full of fuel. Here is a little story about our tent.

SUPER TENT

At K2 our living quarters were winterized tents. I know I shouldn't bitch, but we froze our asses off when it got cold. If any ground pounders are reading this please forgive me for being such a candy ass, but you know how the Air force pampers their people. I can remember lying in my rack with everything I owned piled over me and under me and still freezing! Anyhow, there were a couple of guys in the tent that got tired of this and went looking for something to insulate the tent with. They found a whole load of ½ or 3/4in thick, 4ft x 8ft plywood sheets in a storage area somewhere on the base and "midnight requisitioned" a bunch of it. This was really nice stuff. I don't know where they got the tools but they went ahead and lined our tent with the plywood and did a beautiful job. That was the classiest tent on the base, if not in all of Korea! How they did it and didn't get caught is beyond me. A couple of weeks after they finished really "winterizing" the tent we were all moved to Quonset huts across the road. We moved to the Quonsets some time in mid December '51. These were quite nice, but what a blow after all that work.

Down on the flight line our armament area was a series of large tents. It got mighty cold in there when the wind blew, which was most of the time. Over here in Korea we didn't have the indigenous personnel to clean the machine guns like we had in Japan. We had to pull them out of the aircraft, dismantle and clean them, reassemble them and reinstall them in the aircraft. We spent some long days and nights down on that line doing just that. Once we got organized and working in shifts things got a little better. Here are some of the incidents that occurred down on the flight line.

TWO 500'S

Sometime in September '51, it must have been Indian Summer and quite hot, we loaded the F-84's with two 500 lb. bombs and two Jato bottles each. (JATO stands for "Jet Assisted Takeoff." Actually it was Rocket Assisted Takeoff.) Those poor birds were so under-powered they needed rockets to get them off the ground in hot weather. One pilot apparently couldn't fire his Jato bottles so as he approached the end of our 10,000 foot PSP runway he saw he wasn't going to make it, so he jettisoned the two 500 lb. bombs which then proceeded to skid down the runway at well over 100 mph. He probably toggled them off with the arming wires in place but they must have gotten pulled out during their journey. As a result both of the bombs went off and blew the end of the runway off! The airplane was long gone when this happened but our tents, which were fairly close, didn't fair so well. I remember coming into the tent, it was still light outside, and looking up at the tent top! It looked like the stars were out!! It was badly perforated and needed some repair before the next rainstorm.

BAIL OUT

This incident happened in November of 1951. Our F-84s were coming back to K2 from a mission over North Korea, which was always an exciting time on the field. The scuttlebutt was that one of them was badly damaged. I don't know how this news traveled so fast, but it did! Anyhow, most of the undamaged aircraft made their passes and landed. This guy made a low and slow pass so the tower could take a look at him. It didn't look good! One main landing gear was fully up; one was jammed halfway down, as was the nose gear. A landing in this condition would spread the aircraft, and the pilot, all over the field. The word got around that he had been told to eject. He climbed to about 5,000 feet, right over the field, and punched out. We saw the canopy come off and then the pilot come out and saw him separate from the seat and his chute blossom. The seat dropped like a stone. But then an eerie thing happened. The pilotless F-84 began to circle the field as if someone was flying it. It must have made two or three circuits of the field coming lower and lower. East of the field was a range of mountains and on the last downwind pass it caught a wingtip and was gone in a flash! The pilot came down with no problems. All the time this was going on I remember there being a deathly silence on the field, like everyone was holding their breath.

FLYING BLIND

Again, our aircraft were coming back from a mission and we heard that one of them was pretty badly shot up. The F-84 had been hit by ground fire during a bombing run and the pilot had been blinded. His wingman was with him and telling him how to fly the airplane in order to get back to K2! If you are not a pilot you don't realize how difficult it is to do something like that! Anyhow, with the help of his wingman he got back to the field, which was probably the easy part of this terribly difficult situation. The wingman talked him through a low pass, so the tower could check his landing gear, and then talked him through a very good landing! I can't imagine how tight your pucker string must be drawn in a situation like that! We later went over to take a look at the aircraft and could see that it had taken a 20mm round right into the engine intake. There it penetrated some sheet metal and then struck the top edge of the front armor plate in front of the pilot where it exploded. This explosion blew out the right front Plexiglas windshield, which in turn hit the pilot directly in the face. I don't recall if the pilot's eyes were damaged but I did hear that all the blood from the wounds had blinded him. Again, this was quite a feat of airmanship and shows how well trained and gutsy our pilots were.

A very junior US Navy Lt. (jg) Walter M. Schirra, Jr., serving on exchange duty with the 154th FBS, gets strapped into the cockpit of an F-84E Thunderjet at Taegu for a mission over North Korea, with help from Sergeant Harrison, crew chief of the aircraft. Schirra later became one of the original "Mercury Seven" astronauts, and the only astronaut to fly in space in all three major American programs—Mercury, Gemini, and Apollo. *Robert L. Bell.*

K-2, Taegu, Korea. '51-'52

This F-84, from the 111th FBS, sustained damage over N. Korea. A 20mm round came in through the engine intake and exploded on the upper edge of the front armor plate. It blew out the right front plexi windscreen and blinded the pilot who was able to fly back to K-2 and land!

THE MUD WAGON

The "Mud Wagon" was the name the guys lovingly gave to the Red cross weapons carrier that the Red Cross girls drove down the flight line. Twice a day they came, rain or shine, and brought hot coffee and fresh doughnuts, as much as you wanted, to every outfit on the line. They did this seven days a week and were really a bright spot in our day. I can only imagine how often those girls got "hit on" every day! They must have heard every line in the book and then some!

Those girls also had a canteen that was across the field and was open 24 hours a day. Here again they had hot coffee and fresh donuts and games, if you wanted them, and also letter writing materials. It was very nice. When I wrote home and told my mother about the way the Red Cross treated us she immediately went and volunteered to help them out. She kept that up for at least 25 years, cooking in the Red Cross Bloodmobile canteen. That turned out to be quite a payoff for them.

Sometime in early '52, much to our dismay we were to learn, the Red Cross packed up and moved to an airfield closer to the 38th parallel where the fighting had finally stalled. In their place the Air Force brought in Special Services. We thought things would be about the same as they were when the Red Cross was there. We had a sad awakening! No more mud wagon, you had to go to them if you wanted coffee and donuts. AND you better have some cash! Sadly, things were never the same.

HALF PRICE PLATES

This is a funny one, or not so funny, depending on your point of view. There was a Tech Sgt. in the armament section of the 154th, his first name was Charlie, I don't recall his last. He was one of the nicest guys from Little Rock. Some of them were real jerks. Anyhow, Charlie had been in the Air Force during WWII and as I recall had spent quite a bit of time overseas in the South Pacific. When the 154th was activated Charlie, being in the 154th, had to go also. I guess he owned a hardware store and had to sell it as a result. Here is the tragic part, and don't think Charlie wasn't kicking himself day in and day out. He had joined the Air National Guard because he could get his auto license plates for HALF PRICE!! Isn't that something?

TINY TIM

One day we heard the squadron was going to get a special piece of ordinance. Special it was! We got two gigantic boxes and inside the first was, as I recall, a 10.75 inch diameter rocket body about 10 feet long. It also had a slew of small rocket nozzles on the tail end with a long cable hanging out of the center nozzle. In the other box was the 10.75 in warhead which itself was about 3 ft long. This was an experimental air to ground rocket called "Tiny Tim." We carefully assembled the warhead to the body and trundled this assembly out to one of the F-84s and hung it on one of the bomb pylons. This was quite a large assembly hung on that airplane! The long cable at the rear of the rocket was pulled up and put into the bomb arming solenoid. This is how the rocket was ignited. When the rocket was dropped off the bomb pylon the cable stayed with the airplane. The cable spun a magneto, inside the rocket, igniting the charge and off it went! I'm sure we hung two Jato bottles on that bird to help it off the ground. I'm also sure the pilot, whoever he was, was really goosey on takeoff with that big beast hanging underneath the airplane. He did get airborne with no problems and we later heard that he had been sent to attack a bridge with this rocket. We heard that he made his run on the bridge and dropped the rocket off which ignited with much flame and smoke. He said he had no idea where the rocket went but the bridge was still intact when he pulled up from his run. Apparently Tiny Tim was not much of a weapon.

ROK AIR FORCE PERSONNEL

We had a contingent of Republic of Korea Air Force people attached to our armament section at K2. We were supposed to . . . train these people to take over our duties if and when they took over our aircraft. These kids, as far as I was concerned, must have just come off the farm. They couldn't have been more than 15 or 16 years old and none of them seemed to know one end of a screwdriver from the other. In most cases they acted like a bunch of giggling teenagers, which they were. We tried to train them but it turned out to be an exercise in futility.

I'll give you an example. Since our main mission was interdiction, on almost every mission the aircraft carried 500, 1000, and sometimes 2000 pound bombs. These bombs were put in place, on the bomb pylons, using a hydraulic 3 wheel dolly. These bomb pylons on the F-84 were located close to the fuselage at the wing root. Just behind these pylons, on the fuselage, was a dive brake that was always in the down position when the aircraft was on the ground. When wheeling the bombs into place, prior to jacking them up to the shackle, one had to be very careful not to catch the bomb dolly on this dive brake, because with all that weight the dive brake could easily be damaged. I don't care how many times we warned them about that they invariably hit that dive brake! Finally we gave up and just did the loading our selves. (Was there method to their madness?)

Their NCO (non-commissioned officer) in charge was a Korean S/Sgt. about 20 years old. At one point I was in charge of all the ammunition for our squadron and as such had a large tent where we stored literally thousands of rounds of .50 caliber Armor Piercing Incendiary ammo. We also took the ammo and belted it and loaded it into the cans that held the ammo for the four nose guns. (The two wing guns were loaded out on the line.) To do this meant working in the tent and to keep from freezing in cold weather we had a pot bellied stove inside. This was all quite safe if one took proper precautions. I used the ROK air force personnel to perform these duties and they did them quite well. One cold day I came into the tent and found the ROK S/Sgt. entertaining his troops. He had pulled the projectile out of one of the .50 cal rounds and was tossing the powder, which looks like small chunks of hollow pencil lead, on the top of the hot pot bellied stove! The powder would cook off and fly around inside the tent. They were having a great time! I got really upset and proceeded to ream the S/Sgt's butt. I was a Buck Sgt. and that didn't go over too well with him because I guess he lost some face. I explained to him the consequences of having that tent catch fire and the ensuing fire works display, with all that ammo going off in random directions. We probably could have lost some aircraft since we were just across the taxi way from them. Anyhow, I never heard anything about it from my superiors, which surprised me since I fully expected this S/Sgt. to report me for accosting a superior NCO.

We spent about two months in those armament tents down on the flight line before we moved closer to the northern end of the runway. Here we moved into a "gunite" building which served as our armament shack. This was class in comparison to the tents we had been in, and a whole lot warmer!

5 INCH ROCKETS

The armament shack, which was roughly 20ft by 50ft in size, was right on the taxi way across from where they parked the F-84's. The taxiway, was made of PSP (perforated steel planking) and as I recall was about 200 ft wide. That PSP was about 1/8in thick and fairly sturdy. One day there were about 10 or 15 of us in the shack, most of the aircraft were probably out on a mission, when we heard this horrible WHOOSH! Everyone hit the concrete deck. After a few seconds we decided to investigate, so we poured out the door and onto the taxiway. Right across from us, underneath an F-84, lay an armorer being attended to by a buddy. These guys were not from our squadron. Shortly thereafter a meat wagon (ambulance) slid to a stop, loaded this guy onboard, and headed for the base hospital. We talked to the buddy and found out they were checking the continuity of the 5in rockets hung on this F-84 when all of a sudden the one they were checking ignited. The tail fin must have caught the guy that was hurt which may have caused the rocket to pitch down. This is what saved us in the armament shack. Now comes the amazing part. When that rocket pitched down it hit the PSP and punched a hole in it, without going off!! Apparently the nose fuse was still unarmed and the tail fuse did not arm because the rocket had not accelerated enough to cause it to arm. Anyhow, the rocket traveled about 30ft UNDERGROUND before it came up and punched an exit hole in the PSP and then flew right over our shack and out somewhere toward the ammo dump! It never exploded. If that rocket wouldn't have hit that guy we could have all ended up dead! I shiver now just to think of it.

SAME STRETCH

As I have said our primary mission was interdiction. My understanding was that our pilots had to bomb the same stretch of railroad track almost every day. And every day they found that stretch of track back in place and in working condition. I guess they had the "coolies" working all night to fix it. This, as I recall, went on for months. Finally, we got word to start fusing the bombs with delayed action fuses, which, in retrospect, made a whole lot of sense. Why this wasn't done sooner is beyond me. One of the big problems with these delayed action fuses is that if an aircraft comes back with the bombs on board, as a result of a malfunction, the fuses can't be removed since they are built so that if removal is attempted the bomb explodes. I don't ever recall running into that problem, thank goodness.

HIGH ALTITUDE RESCUE

In December of '51 our squadron was returning from a mission over North Korea. They were at high altitude, probably about 40,000 feet, when one of the F-84's went into a dive. The other pilots tried to raise this particular aircraft on the radio, to no avail. Luckily, a characteristic of the F-84 was that when it exceeded sound speed it would pitch up, which this aircraft did. When it stalled and again dove the other pilots knew that this pilot was in some kind of trouble, probably a faulty oxygen system. Two of them dove down to see what they could do. After another pitch-up and dive the two decided at the next pitch-up they, one on each side of the stricken aircraft, would attempt to catch and steady the plane on their wing tips. I don't know if they were successful on their first try but they did succeed and steadying the Thunderjet between them they managed to get this plane to a lower altitude where the pilot came to and was able to fly back and land on his own.

This incident was written up in Life magazine which I have not been successful in locating. By the way, none of the aircraft wing tips were damaged because the air flow over the surfaces prevented contact.

Capt. J. Paladino was the pilot that lost consciousness and Capt. J. Miller and Lt. W. MacArthur were the pilots that rescued him.

By the way there was another pilot in the 154th with a distinctive gold helmet. He was a navy exchange pilot and his name was, and is, Wally Schirra of astronaut fame. I met Wally many years later and told him of my involvement with the 154th and we chatted about those long gone days. He told me that those were some of his best days in the service. I also knew his mom, Florence Schirra. She was quite a lady and had been a wing walker in her younger days.

ONE FOR THE BOOKS!

When the 154th was shipped overseas we were equipped with F-84E's which were the latest at the time of the straight wing F-84's. We had those aircraft from July '51 in Japan until probably December of '51 when we were told to ship all of them up to the north end of the field to the 49th F/B Wing. We were told we would be getting "new" aircraft. You wouldn't believe what showed up! We got old F-84B's and C's that had been in Germany. These aircraft were really tired and in bad shape armament-wise. We heard that the outfits in Germany, that we got this "junk" from, got the latest swept wing F-84F's as replacements. This must have made our pilots feel just great! It's as if the Air Force was saying "Here is some old junk we would like you to get rid of, we can't send you the new stuff, it might get damaged." What a boot in the pants! In my view that is "one for the books."

UNFORGETTABLE

The more I think about this incident the harder it is for me to believe it. One day I was in the barracks about mid-day, which was very unusual. Either I was sick or it was bad weather and all missions were scrubbed. In any case, very seldom was I in the barracks during the day. I was laying in my rack, probably smoking (I'm glad I gave that up), and listening to the radio my brother had sent me shortly before. I was tuned to the Armed Forces Radio Service, listening to all the nice music, when the disc jockey came on and announced that he had a request to play "Unforgettable" by Nat Cole for Sgt. Don Paul, somewhere in Korea, from Florence Budziak (destined to be my bride). I almost fell out of my bunk!! The odds of me hearing that request have got to be astronomical, since normally all my waking hours were spent down on the flight line. To this day that is OUR song.

A PILOT'S VIEWPOINT

This is a letter I got from a pilot, by the name of John Woodall, that was in the 136th about his experiences flying combat missions in the F-84 Thunderjet.

Don; It has been many a year since I flew an F-84D or E. But I remember it as a GREAT aircraft from the survival viewpoint. Yes, it was well built. Like a tank and in the same vein as it's predecessor, the P-47 Thunderbolt which I also flew for a short time stateside and in the Philippines after the end of WWII. And, yes, it was underpowered by later standards, but at the time we didn't think too much of that since it was far more capable than the aircraft it was replacing, the F-80. Think of it as a computer you might have purchased only 6 months ago and look around and find that their power has nearly doubled in that time and you wish you had a new one. But then hardly anyone really has one of those yet and for the most part they are still pretty pictures in the catalog. That is the F-84D/E in 1951. Except for the F-86, which was purely a one-on-one long range escort fighter, it was still the most powerful in the inventory.

I mentioned security: Tops in "Keep you out of trouble, take a lot of punishment and get you home". Who could ask for anything more? Migs? We hardly gave them a thought. We knew that, if you see them you evade them. The only time you encountered Migs was in pulling off bomb runs. This was primarily due to their well justified fear of the F-86s usually sitting up there somewhere (ones that you rarely saw yourself). The Migs would make a single diving pass at you as you pulled up from your run and that would normally be it. I never knew anyone to be hit by one. Some good old Britisher or Aussie apparently was sitting on the end of the runway at Antung, the Chinese Airfield just across the Yalu and he would come in with a "Four off at Antung" and you could look down and see the dust clouds from their t/o blast. Don't know where those guys were, but they had real GUTS.

Yes, a flight would sometimes make a sweeping pass at the formation on way to the target. This in an effort to make us drop our ordnance, but the F-84 could easily turn inside the Mig and in a one-on one it would hardly be a contest, assuming the Mig was foolish enough to hang around for another try. His great advantage was that he could get away whenever he so desired.

Wing tip drop tanks: I personally don't recall anyone with me ever dropping their tanks. Empty, the plane flew just about as well with as without, and if you had passed Pyongyang (that juicy target we were never allowed to disturb) You had better think twice about dropping them unless you enjoyed bailing out on the way back over some less than friendly territory.

Mission: Typical after first month or so: Took off at daybreak or 2:00 PM, climbed to 35,000, flew direct to Northwest coast in area of Sinanju or Sinuiju (both very near China border just below Yalu.), dropped auxiliary tanks after passing beautiful power plant north of Pyongyang which was also a big NO-NO (Can't deprive those nice people of their electricity can we?), began descent to 10,000 feet over the target (always those blasted high tech railroad tracks!) of which they had thousands already assembled in pre-setup sections just like with your toy train set lined for miles along the right-away (And thousands of Chinese laborers in bunkers waiting only for us to leave to replace the damaged sections immediately). Ground fire got pretty heavy from this point on. After all, they knew we were coming and almost exactly when and where because didn't we always do it there at just that time? I only flew 40 missions compared to 100 for the regular pilots, but of those 40, at least 35 were to that same section of track. It always looked in pretty good shape to me. The run itself was normally on a north heading with speed-brake extended. We were in single file with pull-out at 1000 to 500 feet (or lower if you had the guts) then full throttle and sharp breaking climb to the west (to get over the small range along the coast and to safety over the water), join up in climb and head home. Total time out and back about 2 or 2 ½ hours.

In retrospect: The F-84 was a superb airplane for the mission it was assigned. The F-51s were practically wiped out attempting the same job and the F-80s didn't fare much better.

I later flew the F-100D/E and they were also a superb plane for the time and the only one that could really pass Mach 1 in level flight, although you used most of your fuel with the A/B getting it there. But I would not match the latter with the F-84 in a dog-fight if the F-100 was foolish enough to try to get on the tail of the F-84 other than a surprise pass. But then, those tactics are gone forever. Long range guided missiles have put those tactics in the cellar.

Have I left anything out? It was Soooooo—Loooooong ago!

Keep the faith—John Woodall

Here is a story told during one of our bull sessions in the armament shack at K2 while waiting for our planes to return from a mission. It was told by Pete Stull, one of the regulars and a retread from WWII. Pete had been with the Army Air Corps (that's what they called the Air Force then) in England during WWII. He had been an armament man attached to a P-51 outfit. One day, probably May 8, 1945, he was out on the flight line working on the P-51 assigned to him. He said that he had all the wing panels off and all six of the .50 cal. Machine guns pulled out and his tools scattered all over the place. While he was working on this partially disassembled bird he said another GI came riding a bicycle down the line peddling furiously and shouting at the top of his voice "the war is over, the war is over!" Pete said he got down off the airplane wiped his hands and slowly walked back to the barracks and never looked back. He never went back to the flight line and for all he knew that airplane, with all his tools, is still sitting there, partially disassembled, to this day (in 1951).

Chapter 10

TACHIKAWA, JAPAN
YOKOHAMA, JAPAN

SOME PHYSICAL

I AND A bunch of other GI's arrived at Tachikawa AFB, not far from Tokyo, about mid-May 1952. We were here for processing on our way back Stateside. I had come by a rickety sleeper train from Fukuoka, Japan, down on the island of Kyushu. We were all billeted in the local barracks waiting for whatever was to happen next.

There was an announcement that the next morning we would all be given physicals prior to being moved up to Yokohama where we would board our ship taking us across the Pacific to the States.

The next morning after breakfast the whole bunch of us were marched over to the local gymnasium where we were lined up outside in a single file. There were a lot of people in this line; the best that I can remember is there must have been about 500 of us. Again we were told that we would be getting physicals after which we were free to go to lunch. I was having a hard time figuring out how they could give physicals to all of these people

MY SHORT (BUT EXCITING) TIME WITH THE MILITARY

in such a short period of time. The only exam I remembered was the one prior to being inducted and that took all day.

Anyhow, one by one we inched up to the door of the gymnasium, which opened into a small vestibule. Once inside we were told to strip down to our GI shoes and carry our clothes on our arm. There was another door in the vestibule leading into the gym proper. Just inside that door was a small table with one guy sitting at it taking names and serial numbers and another standing with a fist full of tongue depressors. I guess they were Medics. As you moved up in line he took a tongue depressor and looked into each individual's mouth. Then we were ordered to walk down to the other end of the gym, which by the way was totally empty!

There at the other end of the gym was another station identical to the first, two Medics and a small table. Here you were given a "short arm inspection" and then told to get dressed. While dressing I looked back into this cavernous gym and saw the longest "peter parade" I had ever seen in my life! Men of all sizes and shapes some well and some not so well endowed. What a sight that was! Too bad the days of integrated sexes in the military came along so late.

I finally understood how they could examine so many people in such a short time. If you didn't have "hoof and mouth disease" you got to proceed to Yokohama. Fortunately I passed the test.

ON TO YOKOHAMA

For some reason, when it came time to go on to Yokohama, I was chosen as part of the "advance party" and so we left a day early. When we arrived at the harbor in Yokohama, that same day, we boarded the ship with all of our gear.

The ship we were to cross the vast Pacific on was the USNS Sultan. As advance party we were taken below decks and told to find a bunk. The compartment I ended up in was toward the stern of the ship and I would find out the implications of that when we were out to sea. In this compartment the bunks, as I recall, were stacked four (4) high. There was not much room between you and the guy above you. Once we were settled in we were given free reign of the ship, almost. The upper decks, above the main deck and amidships, were reserved for officers and their families which was almost half the ship, the best half! At this point in time the ship was quite empty and roaming about on deck was easy.

I had gotten chummy with a fellow by the name of Juan Smith, from the 154th, that was rotating Stateside at the same time as I. Juan was from Little Rock, AK, was part American Indian, and looked Jewish, quite a combination. We spent a lot of time leaning on the rail and looking over the wharf and the harbor. The weather was beautiful, sunny and warm.

During the afternoon of that first day some sailors, about five of them, came down the dock carrying their sea bags, and what appeared to be brand-new Samsonite luggage that they probably had purchased at the commissary. Juan and I were on deck just above the gangway when these "swabbies" attempted to come aboard. There was a navy Petty Officer at the end of the gangway who was there to "check in" boarding personnel. The PO would not allow these sailors on board with their new luggage. No matter how much they argued his answer was always the same. "No civvie luggage on board!!" Finally the sailors gave up and grudgingly emptied their newly acquired luggage and stuffed all their gear into their sea bags. Now, what to do with this beautiful luggage? They all began trying to destroy it as best they could!! That stuff is tough! They were jumping up and down on it, bashing it on the pilings, and anything else they could think of! Finally, after doing as much damage as they could, they heaved it off the end of the dock into the bay. What a shame!

Anyhow, it all finally sank. In no time there were small Japanese boats with hard hat divers on the scene and they went down and recovered the now damaged and somewhat soggy luggage. Here is the ironic part. Not too long after this incident happened a taxi came down the wharf and out stepped a Chief Petty Officer in his dress blues with stripes up and down both arms, he must have been in the Navy forever. Not only did he have a sea bag; he also had civvie luggage and a giant sea chest! The boarding officer said not a word to him about what he could and could not bring aboard. Not only that but also this CPO strolled on board carrying not one piece of his gear. Shortly thereafter some swabbies from the ship went and brought his gear on board! Rank has it's privileges!!

On that same day, later in the afternoon, an announcement came over the PA system that all lower three graders, that's Pvt. up to and including Sgt., which is me, should remove their gear from the area I was in and move it to another area. I guess they wanted only top three grades in that compartment. I decided not to move and no one in that bay complained about it so I stayed. I figured that they were grouping all the lower grades in certain bays in order to find people for s—t details, such as KP. So far so good.

Later that day we were told that we could have shore leave, so Juan and I headed into Yokohama. We were told to be back aboard ship at 2400 hours, midnight, at the latest. We hit all the local bars and cabarets downtown and managed to drink up all of our money. It was getting late and we had no idea where we were. We decided to pawn something in order to get a cab back to the waterfront. But, what to pawn? I had a nice ring that Juan said would be a good candidate and I said definitely not! I'm sure he had something that I said would be just as good and he also declined. So, what to do? We hailed a cab and got in and started to bargain. Finally it came down to a Japanese Zippo type lighter that I had had for quite some time. The cabby looked at it and said no but when I showed him something uniquely nasty about it he hastily agreed.

Now we had to try and explain where we wanted to go, which proved to be rather difficult. Finally I drew him a picture of a boat and he got the flash immediately. We arrived at dockside just before 2400 hours. Saved by the lighter!

Chapter 11

THE BOUNDING MAIN

THE FOLLOWING DAY a whole slew of GI's arrived and boarded the ship. There must have been a couple of thousand of Army, Air Force, and Marines that boarded along with quite a few officers and their families. The next day we got under way and headed out of Yokohama harbor and out into the Pacific headed for the good old USA!

The first days were quite nice, sunny, warm, and calm. However, on about the third or fourth day it started to get rough with high seas and wind. If you recall I had said I was billeted in a bay close to the stern. While sailing through these high seas the ship would pitch up and down as we met the waves head on. When it would pitch down the screws (propellers) would lift out of the water and the whole ship would shudder and vibrate!! I was sleeping, or trying to, right where this was happening! This went on for about four days.

I have never been prone to any kind of motion sickness so I was having no problem. Some of the guys were not so fortunate and were spending much of their time trying to heave up their innards! The word was out that if you were bending over the rail and heaving and you felt something hairy in your mouth, don't spit it out because it was your a—hole! Finally the sea calmed and the rest of the trip was nice and smooth. As I recall our "Luxury Cruise" took about seventeen days.

Most of our time was spent in our bunks reading or in the main wardroom, located in about the center of the ship below decks. A lot of the action there was in the card games, poker and such. I avoided those like the plague. A lot of guys got cleaned out in those games. Two swabbies were running a fairly legitimate game of "poker bingo." You "bought" one or more bingo cards with card faces instead of numbers, at a buck per card. Then the two swabbies, one dealing and one watching, peeled the cards off a deck and called them out and you matched the cards on your card(s). They took 10% of the ante for every hand or if less than 10 cards were out they took a buck. Those two guys had a roll of money big enough to choke a horse! I'm sure they made themselves a nice piece of change in the 17 days it took us to cross the Pacific.

On the nice days you could go up on deck, and if you could find a spot on the deck, lie down and snooze in the sun. The main deck was blocked in the center of the ship by the upper deck superstructure. So we GI's had the fore deck and the after deck for our use. It could really get crowded!

The upper deck superstructure was where the officers and their families were billeted. The officers dining area was on the same level as the main deck and had windows where we GI's pressed our noses and watched how the "upper crust" dined in splendor! They really had it nice, with rug on the floor, white tablecloths, and waiters. That was first class! Some of the officer's dependents were young ladies around the age of 18 or so. There was a lot of drooling going on outside those windows! There was one young lady I recall in particular. She would go up on the upper deck, one deck up from the main deck where all us yahoos were, and stand by the rail looking aft and letting her skirt swirl up around her long legs. She was a cutie and knew it! There were some mighty lascivious thoughts

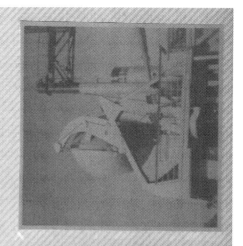

ON BOARD USNS SULTAN BAND
FOR SAN FRANCISCO FROM
YOKOHAMA, JAPAN

JOHN SMITH

swirling around down on that deck with the GI's!! That young lady knew exactly what she was doing!

I think it was on about the fourth day out of Yokohama and I had wandered down to the main wardroom to check out the action. I spotted this large group of guys standing about in the center of the bay and so I went over to see what was going on. Talk about curiosity killing the cat! I was standing on tip toe out on the periphery of the group trying to see what was going on when all of a sudden they parted and there I was standing, facing an officer seated at a table. He asked me name and rank and then & there I was assigned to KP for the rest of the voyage!! All my hard work trying to avoid work details went right down the drain in the blink of an eye! Oh well, I did eat well for the rest of the trip. No more sleeping in 'till 5am any more, it was up at 4am to get ready for breakfast!

What I found to be curious was that the prisoners on board ate first. I hadn't even known we had prisoners on board. They ranged from petty thieves all the way up to murderers. I guess they were all headed to Leavenworth, KS military prison to do hard time making little ones out of big ones.(hard labor breaking rocks). The one murderer was an Army GI that came back to Japan from Korea only to find his Japanese girl friend shacked up with a new love. I guess he killed them both. How stupid can you get? Another prisoner was an Air Force pilot that had supposedly sold his parachute on the black market to get a few bucks. Another brilliant move! In all there must have been about 50 to 75 prisoners and when they were brought in to the galley it was at gunpoint. All the military police guarding these guys had their weapons out and ready. I guess the prisoners could have rioted and taken over the ship. Where would they go, North Korea?

Our KP days were fairly long, starting at about 4am and ending about 7pm or so depending on how long it took us to clean up after the last meal.

We did have some time to ourselves in between meals. Usually I headed straight for my bunk for some shuteye and recoup for the next day.

One morning, very early, probably around 2am, all the KP's were rudely awakened and told to report to the galley. We couldn't figure out what the problem could be or what we had done wrong! As it turned out the officer in charge of the galley was Italian and was so pleased with our performance he had baked up a bunch of Pizzas and had brought us down for a treat! As far as I was concerned a better treat would have been to just let us sleep and so I wandered back to my bunk and crashed for a few more hours.

We had some beautiful sunsets out in the middle of the Pacific! We also had some very large birds that followed us all the way across. All day they would fly in our wake, I guess waiting for the garbage to be tossed overboard. At night they would land on the fantail rail and roost all night. All the way across the Pacific I don't recall seeing another ship or an island or anything, other than those birds.

One evening, late in the voyage, the scuttlebutt had it that we were going to be coming into San Francisco bay the next morning. It turned out to be June 4th, my birthday!! What a great present! We were awakened early and it was still dark when we were approaching the Golden Gate Bridge. We could just make the bridge out ahead of the ship as we slipped through the dark waters of the mouth of the bay. Everyone on board was on deck and no one was talking as I recall. It was deathly quiet and all that could be heard was the thrumming of the engines and the water lapping against the hull as we silently made our way into the bay. Just as we passed under that beautiful bridge all hell broke loose on board that vessel, with everyone shouting and screaming as loud as they could!! What a present!! Unfortunately then it was back to KP.

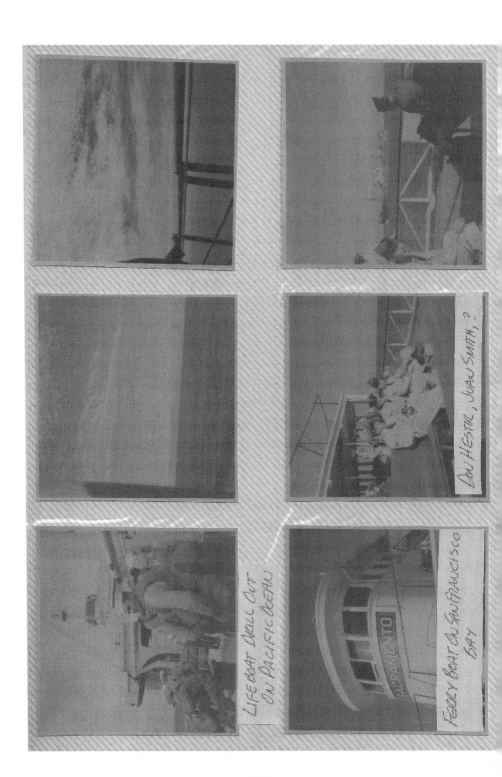

Don Hester, Juan Smith, ?

Life Boat Drill Out on Pacific Ocean

Ferry Boat on San Francisco Bay

That morning we tied up to a dock on Treasure Island or Yerba Buena, which is an old Navy base located in the center of the bay, and started to disembark. I can remember walking on that concrete pier and feeling it roll and pitch, just like the ship. It was just my imagination and the fact I had been on a ship for so long. Once ashore we were given billets and started our processing for distribution to other bases. All our records were checked and we were given the choice of going to a local Air Force base, Hamilton AFB north of San Francisco, for discharge or going to the base closest to home. Unfortunately I chose the latter.

They only had a skeleton crew on Treasure Island and so, during our stay there, which lasted about 5 or 6 days, we were used to do everything around the base. S—t details to be more precise! I even saw M/Sgts. sweeping the streets! They must have enjoyed that!!

On our voyage I had pulled on a toenail and it had become infected. I was treating it with after shave lotion, mostly alcohol, but not having much luck. One morning I decided to go on sick call since I was getting tired of the crap details we were getting. When the corpsman looked at the toe he almost panicked and started to look for a red line running up my leg and feeling the lymph nodes in my groin. He said I was on the verge of blood poisoning! I had just come in to avoid the work details. After giving me a healthy shot of penicillin he told me to report back in a few days, which I did and all was well.

Not too long after arriving I got to a phone and called home. The phone call to Flo lasted for an hour and must have cost a fortune. Long Distance calls in those days were mighty expensive. I did reverse the charges. Luckily Flo was working for the Phone Company and her boss took care of the charges.

That trip to sick bay almost got me in a lot of trouble. When we were in line on the last day to receive our travel papers and my name was called I was told to report for extra duty. The extra duty would have been to stack the mattresses of all the guys that had just been processed. What a bummer!!! When I asked why, I was told I had missed muster one morning and this was to be punishment for that infraction. I told them I was on sick call and got nothing but the "fish eye." They said there was no indication of any "sick call" on their records. I really had to scramble and got over to the medics and hunted up the corpsman that had taken care of me. After much cajoling on my part he reluctantly agreed to come and talk to the "powers that be" on my behalf. They listened and they too reluctantly gave me my travel orders. Whew, that was close.

During the stay on Treasure Island we were allowed passes and so three of us went into San Francisco for a little fun. We ended up in a bar on the infamous Barbary Coast and decided to have a few drinks. It wasn't long before two of the girls working in the place were firmly ensconced at our table. This place was a real dump and we three were almost the only people in there. The girls were supposed to be sisters and took turns up on the stage entertaining the few customers that were there. The watered down drinks were coming fast and furious. The girls were beckoning the waiter every time they switched places on the stage. So, I for one ran out of money in a hurry! One more drink showed up and I told this girl at the table that I had no more money. She quickly got up and left and I figured I was going to have some real "fun" with the waiter when he asked for payment. Just as the waiter showed up so did this girl. What came next totally stunned me. As she sat down she nudged my knee and under the table she passed me a twenty dollar bill! I couldn't believe it! She "saved my bacon."I settled the bill, which was the best part of the $20 and we beat it out of there before we ended up in an alley with lumps on our heads! I did thank the girl for her generosity. It was good to be back in the good old US of A!!

Chapter 12

BACK IN THE U.S. OF A.!
HOMEWARD BOUND

SINCE I HAD chosen to travel to the base closest to home for discharge the next thing to do was make travel arrangements to get there. I decided to take the train. I figured that flying was a little riskier and why push my luck at this stage of the game. There was another guy from the ship that decided to do the same thing, and he was headed in the same direction, so we went and bought our train tickets. For $55 each we got a chair car and according to the agent we would have Club Car privileges. What a deal! We were to travel from Oakland to Chicago and then part company. I had a connection to go to Mt. Clemens, Michigan from Chicago and then on to Selfridge Field, which was close to Mt. Clemens.

We left Oakland one morning and headed out, by train, across the US, destination Chicago, IL. As I recall the trip took about 3 days. Not much fun in a chair car but we had survived worse.

The first night my buddy and I went hunting for the Club Car. We did find it and settled down to partake of a few beers. Not too long after beginning our first brew two conductors started coming through the car. One of them was a Pullman conductor and he came to us and asked to see our tickets. Once he had examined them he angrily told us to essentially "get the hell out of his car since it was a Pullman club car and that we had no business being there" and then he abruptly left!! We had no idea.

The guy that I was with had a reputation for being a hot head and I could see he was really getting upset. This same guy had reportedly "taken apart" a bar in Japan after getting upset. Luckily the second conductor saw what was going on and tried to calm this guy down. He explained that the car was for Pullman passengers only and if everyone from the train came and used it there would be no room for the Pullman folks. Made sense.

He told us to take our time and finish our beers and then leave. This smoothed things over and we followed his instructions.

Other than that incident I don't remember much of the train journey back across the U.S.. I do recall the dining car and not having very good service. I did overhear the black waiters talking and I heard one say he didn't like waiting on the GI's because they didn't tip well enough. Too damn bad!

I do remember the train terminal in Chicago, it was gigantic, and seeing a famous comedian there. I'll remember his name one of these days. (It was Fred Allen.)

I finally arrived at Selfridge Field and started my processing for discharge. I soon found out that I had made a big mistake not opting to be discharged on the West Coast at Hamilton AFB. These guys here were like "Molasses in January" when it came to paperwork. Talk about pokey!

Anyhow, the processing was to take about a week and in the meantime it was back to crap details again. Luckily I didn't have to pull any KP but I did get guard duty. I had to guard prisoners from the stockade while they pulled weeds and I watched them while holding an unloaded shotgun!

Well, the week finally came to an end and I was ready to get the heck out of there. I went in to get my orders and money and was told they had lost the paperwork! I almost went through the ceiling! Luckily I had done a favor for one of the guys in the office and he had said he owed me one. I found him and reminded him that he did indeed owe me and he reluctantly said he would help. He typed up new orders and I walked them through the system and got them all signed off in one day! I was on my way to Cleveland the next day, as a civilian.

Again I took the train and I can remember pulling into the station in the Terminal Tower in Cleveland, Ohio. When I got off the train the whole family was there, Mom, Dad, my brother Bob, and uncles and aunts. I do remember Flo standing way in the back as I greeted everyone. I remember that I couldn't take my eyes off of her, she looked so beautiful. Then I finally got to her and we hugged and kissed and all was well.

And so my 21 months in the U. S. Air Force came to an abrupt end. As everyone who has ever been in the armed forces says "It was quite an experience and I don't regret it but I would never want to repeat it."

HEADQUARTERS
575TH AIR BASE GROUP
SELFRIDGE AIR FORCE BASE, MICHIGAN

SPECIAL ORDERS)   E X T R A C T   18 June 1952
NUMBER   108)

21. S SGT ARMAND V CIMIKERS, AF13282526, 575th Ops Sq, 575th AB Gp this
base is reld fr asgmt & dy with 575th Ops Sq, 575th AB Gp this base (ADC EADF)
eff 1 Jul 52 on which dt he is Hon Dischd by reason of ETS. Amn WP his home of
rec 1601 Morris St Philadelphia Pa or place no further dis. PCS. TDN. 5723500
248-401 P534.1-02,03,07 S99-999. Auth: AFR 39-10 & Msg AFPMP-4 ALMAJCOM 78/52
dtd 24 Apr 52.

22. S SGT DAVID McKEE, AF13282553, 575th Ops Sq, 575th AB Gp this base
is reld fr asgmt & dy with 575th Ops Sq, 575th AB Gp this base (ADC EADF) eff
1 Jul 52 on which dt he is Hon Dischd by reason of ETS. Amn WP his home of rec
3238 N Hurley St Philadelphia Pa or place no further dis. PCS. TDN. 5723500
248-401 P534.1-02,03,07 S99-999. Auth: AFR 39-10 & Msg AFPMP-4 ALMAJCOM 78/52
dtd 24 Apr 52.

23. A/1C DONALD J PAUL, AF23580133, this base WP his home of rec 4221
W 50th Cleveland Ohio or place no further dis at such time as w/enable him to
arr thereat on 19 Jun 52 on which dt he is reld fr asgmt & dy with Hq Sq, 575th
AB Gp this base (ADC EADF) and fr EAD. Eff 20 Jun 52 amn is asgd Hq VRS 1st
AF Mitchel AFB NY. PCS. TDN. 5723500 248-401 P534.1-02,03 S99-999. Auth:
AFR 39-14 & Msg Hq USAF AFPMP-4 36222 dtd 29 Nov 51.

BY ORDER OF LIEUTENANT COLONEL JOHNSTON:

OFFICIAL: T W BLACKBURN JR
                                                       Captain   USAF.
                                                       Adjutant

RUSSELL W GETCHEL
CWO   USAF
Asst Adjutant

DISTRIBUTION: "A" & "B" PLUS: 5-CO Hq, VRS, 1st AF Mitchel AFB NY

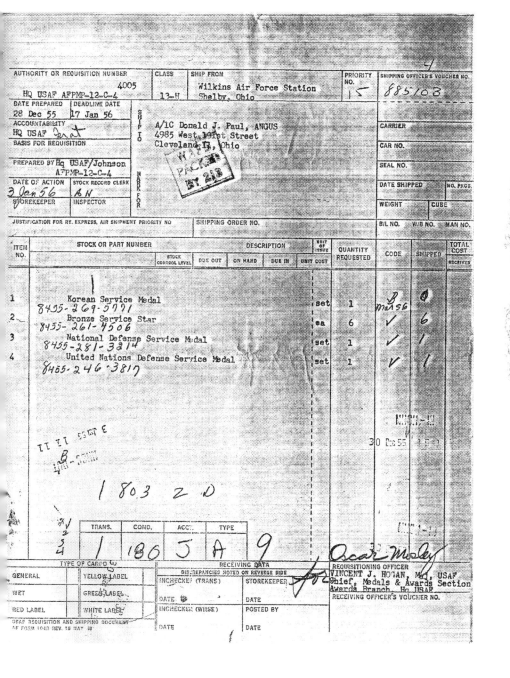

AUTHORITY OR REQUISITION NUMBER		CLASS	SHIP FROM		PRIORITY NO.	SHIPPING OFFICER'S VOUCHER NO.
HQ USAF AFPMP-12-C-4	4005	13-H	Wilkins Air Force Station Shelby, Ohio		5	885103

DATE PREPARED	DEADLINE DATE		SHIP TO			
28 Dec 55	17 Jan 56		A/1C Donald J. Paul, ANGUS 4985 West 191st Street Cleveland, Ohio		CARRIER	
ACCOUNTABILITY HQ USAF					CAR NO.	
BASIS FOR REQUISITION					SEAL NO.	
PREPARED BY Hq USAF/Johnson AFPMP-12-C-4					DATE SHIPPED	NO. PKGS.
DATE OF ACTION 3 Jan 56	STOCK RECORD CLERK BN				WEIGHT	CUBE
STOREKEEPER	INSPECTOR					

JUSTIFICATION FOR RY. EXPRESS, AIR SHIPMENT PRIORITY NO	SHIPPING ORDER NO.	B/L NO.	W/B NO.	MAN NO.

ITEM NO.	STOCK OR PART NUMBER	STOCK CONTROL LEVEL	DUE OUT	ON HAND	DUE IN	UNIT COST	DESCRIPTION	UNIT OF ISSUE	QUANTITY REQUESTED	CODE	SHIPPED	TOTAL COST / RECEIVED
1	Korean Service Medal 8455-269-5771							set	1	Mar 56	0	
2	Bronze Service Star 8455-261-4506							ea	6	✓	6	
3	National Defense Service Medal 8455-281-3214							set	1	✓	1	
4	United Nations Defense Service Medal 8455-246-3817							set	1	✓	1	

30 Dec 55

1 803 Z D

	TRANS.	COND.	ACC'T.	TYPE	
	1	186	J	A	9

Oscar Mosley

TYPE OF CARGO		RECEIVING DATA		REQUISITIONING OFFICER
GENERAL	YELLOW LABEL	DISCREPANCIES NOTED ON REVERSE SIDE		VINCENT J. HOGAN Maj, USAF
		INCHECKER (TRANS)	STOREKEEPER	Chief, Medals & Awards Section
WET	GREEN LABEL			Awards Branch, Hq USAF
		DATE	DATE	RECEIVING OFFICER'S VOUCHER NO.
RED LABEL	WHITE LABEL	INCHECKER (WHSE)	POSTED BY	
USAF REQUISITION AND SHIPPING DOCUMENT AF FORM 1040 REV. 15 MAY 48		DATE	DATE	

- 213 -

TO ALL WHOM IT MAY CONCERN

STATE OF OHIO
OFFICE OF THE ADJUTANT GENERAL

This is to certify that the records of this office show that

DONALD JACK PAUL

enlisted in 112th Bomb Sq.

Ohio National Guard, *on the* 19 *day of* September 19 47, *at*

Cleveland , *Ohio, for the period of* 3 *years.*

Honorably Discharged 8 September 1950 per Expiration Term of Service
Reenlisted 19 September 1950 for 3 yrs Det D 206th Air Sv Grp
Inducted into active military service of the US 25 September 1950
Released from active mil sv of the US and transferred to Inactive Air
National Guard 19 June 1952.

Honorably Discharged 2 July 1953 by reason of discontinuance of Inactive
Air National Guard

Adjutant General

Columbus, O., 14 February 19 55 .

Chapter 13

FORT BENNING, GA—REVISITED

ON ONE OF our many road trips back east from California, in our motor home, we found ourselves in the Columbus, GA area. As I recall it was probably in the year 2000 or so and we were on our way back home. We found a very nice state park not far from Columbus, GA and close to the town of Hot Springs, GA. This is the town where president Roosevelt used to visit frequently to bathe in the hot springs to hopefully help with his Polio.

We did visit his home there and took a tour. I was struck with the fact that, though nice, the home he had there was not in the least ostentatious. It actually was quite small.

Since we were very close to Fort Benning we decided to visit. This base is an "open" base in that civilians are allowed to enter and leave as often as they like. We drove our tow vehicle, our trusty '98 Honda, and entered the base.

Fort Benning is called "The Infantry Center of the World." Armed forces from all over the globe come here to train.

Since it had been fifty years since I had been here I thought it would be a good idea to check into the headquarters building and get some directions. That turned out to be a good idea. The female GI that we talked to gave us directions and also a large map.

Off we went with me trying to remember land marks and using the map to try and find our way. I was able to spot the giant "Jump Towers" that the paratroopers used in their basic training. There were, and are, three of them and they rise up at least a couple hundred feet in the air. The paratroopers are hauled up to the top of the towers, with their parachutes open, and then released. There are four stations on each tower and, depending on wind direction, only two or three of the stations are used so the paratroopers don't drift into the towers while descending.

From the Jump Towers I thought I had a good chance of finding my old area. The only thing I did find was Lawson Field where we had hangers on the flight line and worked on the B-26s. Everything else was gone, our old barracks, our workshops, the local branch of the PX, everything! What did I expect? After all it had been at least fifty years. The barracks that we had occupied were from WWII and were probably so Termite ridden that they fell down!

We drove around the area for a while and I couldn't find anything that I recognized. I was disappointed but at least I had given it a try. On the way out of the base we did stop at the Main PX and looked around. Even it had changed drastically from what I remembered. I tried to buy a post card but was told that since I was not current military I was prohibited from buying anything. And I was too old at the time to reenlist, so I left empty handed.

My revisit to Fort Benning had turned out to be a "bust" but I was glad I had given it a try.

Trying to relive the "good old days" can sometimes be quite frustrating.

Chapter 14

KOREA IN A NUTSHELL

9/9/00 TO 9/17/00

THIS TOUR BACK to Korea after 50 years did not have an auspicious beginning. We signed up for this tour with a company called "Military Historical Tours" based in Virginia. (During the tour I would begin calling this company "Military Hysterical Tours" which will become evident later on in the narrative.") For one reason or another it was on again, off again. But that's another story.

Our trip began at Los Angeles International Airport where, after a lengthy wait, we boarded our Korean Air 747-400, along with many of our fellow tour members. We were traveling to Korea specifically to commemorate the 50th Anniversary of the beginning of the Korean War that began on June 25, 1950. Our group consisted of a majority of Marines and then Army and Navy and finally a few Air Force types, which included me. My wife Florence was accompanying me but with some misgivings. The thought of visiting the Orient had never been high on her priority list. Little did I know that this trip would reinforce those feelings.

After about twelve butt numbing hours we landed in Seoul, Korea, up close to the 38th parallel. (However, this was a far cry from the 36 hours it had taken me to fly to Japan in 1951.)It was now September 10th since we had lost a day crossing the International Date Line. Much to our surprise and enjoyment we were met by a full Honor Guard of Korean Military, all in their best class A uniforms, along with their officers. There were twenty men, bearing arms, and at attention as we passed through their gauntlet. At the end of the gauntlet was hung a large banner, which said "Welcome, Thank You Korean War Veterans." It was a very pleasant and heart warming experience.

We weren't done flying just yet. We were bussed over to another terminal and boarded a flight to Pusan, down on the southern tip of Korea. Fortunately this was a short flight. The day was clear and sunny, one of the few we would see in Korea. In Pusan we were taken to the Paradise Hotel which was really very beautiful. These lodgings would spoil us for the rest of the trip. We were on the 10th floor and had a beautiful view of the beach and ocean.

After a fairly restful night we awoke to a rainy day on the 11th. As it turns out we were on the fringe of a Typhoon which slowly cruised up the Korean peninsula all the time we were there. When it wasn't drizzling it was pouring! Our first day consisted of touring old battlefields and monuments which was done mostly for the Marines and Army among us. We visited the island of Koje-do, which was a very large POW (Prisoner of War) camp for North Koreans during the war. We also toured Syngman Rhee's villa. He was the first president of South Korea following WWII.

On the 12th we visited the Pusan Tower which gave us quite a view of the city and harbor. Many of the men on the tour had landed here not too long after hostilities began in 1950. As I recall none of them could recognize anything! Things do change in 50 years as I was going to find out in a few days. We visited the United Nations Cemetery, which by the way is the only one in the world. There were many GIs buried there from all the countries that fought under the auspices of the UN. We held a commemorative wreath laying in the small chapel on the grounds.

After leaving the cemetery we boarded our busses and headed for Taegu. Little did we know that we were in for a long and tedious trip. As it turned out we were making this journey during the Korean holiday of Cho-Suk which is comparable to our Thanksgiving. All Koreans, and I mean ALL of them, during this holiday are on the road to visit either their relatives or to honor their ancestors.

The distance from Pusan to Taegu is about 90 miles by road. Fifty years ago I'm sure this was a two-lane dirt road but today it is a two lane, each way, divided expressway. I do believe the whole populace of Korea was on this very road. Our travel time was 9 hours and 45 minutes. Do the math. Needless to say we were a very unhappy bunch of travelers by the time we arrived in Taegu. I'm sure the rain didn't help the travel time and it surely didn't help our dispositions! To top it off the hotel we were in in Taegu was early "flop house." Thankfully we only had to spend one night there.

Since this road trip had taken so long our bus thankfully had made many "pit stops" along the way. Unfortunately, in the case of our women, the toilet facilities were mostly Korean. I'll explain. A Korean toilet in not much more than a hole in the floor with places to put your feet. For the women this entails squatting, not much fun for our elderly women and in some cases impossible! We finally did discover, about halfway through the trip, that on each end of the row of Korean toilets was an American type toilet, much to the delight of our ladies.

The next morning, the 13th again in the rain, Flo and I started off on a little adventure of our own out to K2, the airbase where I spent 9 months from September '51 to May of '52 during the war. The base is now called Taegu Air Base. This was not part of the tour but the tour group had promised me a visit. When I approached the tour leader, a retired Marine Col. by the name of Warren Weedham, and told him of the promise I had gotten from his people concerning a visit to K2, he feigned ignorance. I was not about to be denied! He was about to walk away from me when I held his arm and pressed my case! Grudgingly he dug into his pocket and brought out some Korean money so we could hire a taxi. Thank you sooo much Col!

Outside the hotel we found a taxi which took us to the Main Gate of K2 and dropped us off. Due to the holiday the base was almost deserted. There were two Korean Air Force enlisted men manning the gate which we tried to communicate with, to no avail. Luckily arrangements had been made for our Air Force people to meet us and shortly they showed up and got us into the base. There was a T/Sgt., by the name of Graves, and a S/Sgt., by the name of Musgrove. They took Flo and I in a small van to the headquarters building where we met Major Cox. We had a short visit there and I showed them a bunch of pictures I had brought with me showing what life was like at K2 during the war 50 years prior. The Major was impressed with the photos so I gave him the whole lot. He said he was going to put them on the bulletin board for all the troops to see.

As a courtesy the Major offered to drive us around the base so I could try and find some of my "old haunts." As it turned out I couldn't recognize a thing! What did I expect after 50 years? Not only that but for some reason they had a plastic fabric on the fence that surrounds the field. This material was about 6 feet high and was impossible to see through or over. I couldn't believe how things had changed. Where there was nothing but scrub and dirt 50 years ago there now were trees and bushes and greenery everywhere.

We drove up on a small hill on the East side of the field where the ROK (Republic of Korea) Air Force has its headquarters in a beautiful building. From there I could see most of the runway, which is now two parallel concrete runways. In the good old days it was one PSP (Perforated Steel Planking) runway. The runway heading is 31/13 so I was close with my original guess.

Since it was quite overcast and still raining I was having trouble identifying landmarks to the West. I just went ahead and took pictures and was able to identify some of the hills after I got home and processed my pictures.

The ROKAF (Republic of Korea Air Force) shares the field with commercial airlines so they have a civilian terminal there, which I never saw. The Main Gate to the base is to the West as is the city of Taegu. Taegu was not visible from K2 50 years ago. The city has grown so much it has now enveloped the base and goes on beyond it out to the East. There was a small village to the North East that I took a picture of, many moons ago, and it was, at that time, all mud huts with thatched roofs. Now it is all high rise apartments! The rain really put the kibosh to my picture taking. In driving around I think I may have found the area where our Quonset huts were but it was so different I really couldn't tell. All in all the K2 visit was somewhat of a bust but I wouldn't have missed it for anything.

We returned to Major Cox's headquarters area and thanked him for his hospitality. The major then gave us unlimited use of his van in order to get back with our group. The two airmen now had the responsibility of getting us back with our tour group. We set off for Camp Carroll where our tour leader said our group would be spending the day. When we arrived there the group was nowhere to be found. After hunting around the base our driver finally found someone with the MP's (Military Police)that said the group had headed out to another area down the road about 7 miles. After about 20 miles we found an area that looked right. Our driver ran in and got some more information on the location of our group. Off we went again following a military caravan.

It was still pouring rain. At this last destination we finally hit paydirt. We recognized our busses and after a little search found the group. Flo was really upset and was ready to tear into our tour leader, our illustrious Col., but true to his officer training sloughed us off. We each got box lunches, yum yum, and after profusely thanking our airmen, that had driven us all over "hells half acre" to find the group, boarded the busses and were off to Pusan. It had taken us over 3 hours to hunt down our group because the schedule was changing from minute to minute! The trip back to Pusan was a piece of cake in comparison to the trip up, only 5 ½ hours!

At the Paradise Hotel we had dinner in the coffee shop. Flo had noodle soup and I had "flied lice" (fried rice) and Kimchi. Kimchi is a Korean national dish and consists of fermented cabbage and assorted vegetables and is reddish in color. It is somewhat like Sauerkraut with extras thrown in. It normally is quite spicy but can range anywhere from mild to "blow the top of your head off!"

On the 14th we awoke to—more rain. We left the hotel and proceeded to the airport for our flight back to Seoul. When we arrived in Seoul we immediately boarded busses and headed for Inchon, which was not too far. Here we had lunch at an authentic Korean restaurant. After removing our shoes we proceeded to the dining room which was unusual in that each table was set in a pit which is where your legs and feet go. Our chairs were just a padded seat with a back. In the middle of the table was a round covered Hibachi (grill) for cooking meat. When they served the food some of it I could identify and some I could not. The grilled beef was good, as was the beer.

At our table were Navy Captain Bob Schelling and his wife. Very nice people. This gentleman was Captain of the Destroyer USS Swenson that was one of the "Sitting Ducks" during the Marine Inchon landings. I'll explain.

The Inchon landing, which was scheduled for the 15th of September, 50 years prior, was a terrible military gamble at best. The tides in this area run over 30 feet, high to low, making the timing of the assault very important. There is an island there, Wolmi-Do, commanding the harbor. In order to proceed with the landing our military people had to know how heavily fortified Wolmi-Do was. In order to find out what the fortifications on this island were it was decided to send in a flotilla of five destroyers on the 13th & 14th, to draw fire from the island's batteries, or in other words act as "sitting ducks." Not only was there artillery fire to contend with, there were also mines in the harbor to avoid. When in position, about ½ mile from the island, they proceeded to begin a bombardment and fired about 1000 5-inch rounds. The enemy returned fire and scored hits on three of the destroyers including the Swenson. They continued this action until the tide started to go out and they weighed anchor and returned to the ocean. The next day these brave captains and their crews repeated the previous day's action. By the end of the day the fire coming from Wolmi-Do was sparse and intermittent. The harbor was now ready for the invasion on the 15th.

After lunch we attended a wreath laying ceremony commemorating the "Sitting Ducks" which was very stirring.

I have to mention here that all the time we were being moved around by bus in Inchon and Seoul we were given a police escort! No red lights or stop signs for us veterans. How about that?

Following this ceremony we were bussed to the Inchon Metropolitan City Dance Theater to watch traditional Korean Folk Dances put on by the ladies of the Inchon City Dance Company. Beautiful dances and costumes.

That evening, after a short rest, Flo and I attended a dinner at the hotel honoring the Korean War veterans. The meal was very good (round eye (slang for westerners) food-steak) but what surprised most of us was having our names called and one by one going up to the front of the dining room. There we were individually greeted by a high ranking member of the Korean military, in my case a naval officer, and having a medal pinned on my chest, having my hand shaken, and thanked for my service during the Korean War. I was very pleased and Flo was proud. In spite of the weather it was a good day.

On the 15th, after breakfast, we were bussed back to the Inchon Marine Landing Memorial hall and attended a ceremony commemorating those very perilous landings made by the US Marines 50 years prior. Following that we went to a very large Sports Arena and witnessed another commemoration of the Inchon Landings. As we entered the Sports Arena we were each given a small knapsack which had in it our lunch. This consisted of a fat "grease" burger, a container of sweet sour corn, and a dessert. In the arena they had hundreds of people performing as well as many military bands. The local folks were not sparing anything to show us their respect for what we did 50 years ago. I for one was very impressed and pleased. The show lasted about 1 ½ hours.

We again boarded our busses and headed for a high promontory overlooking Inchon Harbor. This area is now called MacArthur Park but 50 years ago it was Telegraph hill and was used by the North Koreans to rain fire down on the invading US Marines. Our next stop was at "Green Beach" which was one of the landing points where the Marines made their initial assault over the sea walls. Not a very hospitable area. Again it was pouring rain. After a short stay there we headed off for a 1 ½-hour bus ride to the DMZ (Demilitarized Zone) which is currently the dividing zone between North and South Korea. On the way to the DMZ we ate our previously issued and now very cold lunches. Here is where we think Flo got into trouble.

Our Korean tour guide told us that 20% of the South Korean GNP (Gross National Product) is currently being spent on defense. (And our people complain about our defense spending!) He also said that the whole shoreline of South Korea is barbed wire! That's comparable to the whole coastline of Florida! The situation there is very tense.

The DMZ is a 5-mile wide "buffer zone" which straddles the demarcation line dividing North and South Korea and stretches from coast to coast. This is a foreboding area, which is desolate for the most part and heavily mined. The roads and bridges are set to be demolished at a moment's notice to stop any armed incursion by the North. As we got into the DMZ we had to exit our busses and board US Army busses which then took us up to Panmunjom. Here is where the armistice talks took place in the '51 to '53 time frame. This area is called the "Joint Security Area." When we exited the bus we entered a large ornate building called "Freedom House." In order to get to the area where the armistice talks took place we had to climb steps up to the second floor, which was really quite high. I guess at this point Flo was really feeling punk and told me to just go ahead and she would wait down below.

I proceeded up the stairs with the group and our GI guide. At the top, and just outside the glassed in area at the rear of the building, we could see the smaller blue buildings where the peace talks had taken place 50 years ago. These buildings are still in use today. As we stood there listening to our guide we could see South Korean GIs standing guard at the south end of these blue buildings. What was odd was their stance. They were at an "at ease" position, feet apart with arms down at their sides, but they were standing with only half of their bodies exposed around the corner of the building. When we asked about this we were told it was done that way to limit the exposure of their bodies to possible gunfire as they stood guard. A tense situation indeed!

These blue buildings, one-story affairs, ran north and south. They were about 100 feet long and 25 feet wide and straddled the demarcation line dividing North and South Korea. A strip of concrete on the ground about 1 foot wide denotes that demarcation line. On the other side of that demarcation line and a few hundred feet inside North Korea was a very large marble building which is called "Panmungak" and is the administrative headquarters of the North Korean Security Force in this Joint security Area. According to our GI guide, although this building is quite large and has three stories, it is only 20 feet or so deep. In other words it is really just a facade much like our western movie sets. On the front steps of this building stood a lone North Korean guard looking at us as much as we were looking at him. Off to the right side of this area stood a large North Korean guard post three stories high.

We were invited to enter the center blue building where the peace talks took place. In the center of the building straddling the demarcation line were large tables where the representatives of the north and south sat facing each other and hammered out the armistice. At one point I was actually standing in North Korea. We then exited this building and reentered Freedom House and proceeded down the stairs heading for our busses. Flo was sitting at a table and was as "white as a sheet." She had gotten sick to her stomach, with the natural result of that, and was being tended to by one of the GI guards. They were concerned enough about her condition to call for an ambulance and wanted her to be taken to see the base doctor. Naturally she was embarrassed and declined the ambulance but promised to see their doctor when we got back to the main area.

Our next stop was an observation station overlooking "The Bridge of No Return." This bridge is where our US POW's (Prisoners of War) were returned to freedom after the armistice was signed. One of the fellows in our group, who had been a POW, said he had come across that very bridge almost 50 years ago. Eerie! Off in the distance was a village that had been put up as a showcase by the North Koreans. I guess the odd thing about it is that it is uninhabited!

When we arrived at the main area the doctor was there waiting for us and took a look at Flo. His diagnosis was that she had picked up a local "bug" and prescribed anti-nausea medication and antibiotics, which he supplied. He promised her that all would be well in 48 hours. The man was true to his word. We re-boarded our busses and proceeded to Seoul. Upon arrival at the Olympia Hotel, in Seoul, there was quite a bit of confusion in getting our room keys. For some reason we were almost the last to get ours. I think there must have been some "hanky panky" because the room we were supposed to get, as shown on the list, had been crossed out and the room we got was not much more that a "closet." It consisted of a small hallway, off of which was the toilet, and ended in a small room. In the room was a chair a small table and a desk. The Queen size bed was jammed in the corner of the room! There was no closet. And we were supposed to spend three days here? It was time to complain!

I hunted up our tour leader and found him in the bar having a drink with some of his cronies. I called him aside and asked if I could see his accommodations. At first he was puzzled but when I told him that our "room" resembled a closet he got the flash. In true military fashion he had me follow him and we proceeded to the lobby where his underlings were still trying to sort things out. He essentially said, "give this man another room" and left. (This guy, our tour leader, was a real jerk!) The story I then got from them was that there were only two other rooms available. Supposedly the hotel was full, a story I found hard to believe. Flo and I went and looked at the other two rooms and decided on the last. At least it did have it's own closet! The morning of the 16th it was again raining. Will it ever stop? Flo was still feeling pretty punk and asked me to bring her some breakfast. After I had breakfast I brought her some tea, toast and Orange juice. It was going to be a busy day so she told me just to go ahead and let her rest for the day. It was probably the best thing for her. She actually slept most of the day. At 0800 (8am) I went down and caught the bus. Our first stop was the Korean Cultural Museum. This was a very beautiful museum and outlined the Korean culture from ancient times up to the current day. Outside the museum on display was a typical thatched roofed mud hut like I remembered seeing 50 years ago. Now most of the population live in high rise apartments.

After spending about two hours soaking up Korean culture we were bussed over to the Korean War Museum. In the entrance to the museum are hung very large brass plaques. On these plaques, arranged by state, are the names of all of the US soldiers that were killed during the Korean War. On the one for the Ohio war dead I found the name of Dave Lasky, a fellow I had gone to high school with. It makes one think! Why him and not me?

This was a very extensive museum and I wish I would have had more time to spend there. According to a chart on one wall the US had contributed 5.72 MILLION people to this conflict. Fortunately the total deaths, about 35,000, were a small percentage of that force. They had a large display of war materiel outside but due to the constant rain I had to pass it up.

Our next stop in Seoul, to please the ladies on the trip, was a shopping area called "Itaewon." The "hucksters" were out in force. Suits, jackets, (tailor made within hours!) and anything else one might want were there for sale. Flo would have had a ball but she was busy snoozing, which was probably the best thing for her condition.

We returned to the hotel a little after 4pm. I had to wake Flo up and she was quite "wiggy" after sleeping most of the day. We were having a "farewell" dinner that evening since some people on the trip were returning to the States while others were continuing on to China. Flo begged off the dinner but I attended. It was a very nice affair with Marine General (Ret.) Bowser as the guest speaker.

General Bowser was with us during our stay in Inchon and Seoul. He apparently was the architect of the Inchon Landings. The General was at this time somewhere in his early 90's. Anytime you saw the General you also saw a Marine Full "Bird" Colonel in tow. I guess the Col. was the General's "baby sitter."

The next morning, the 17th, we packed up, boarded our busses, and headed for Kimpo International Airport (which 50 years ago was K14 and handled most of our F-86s) to get our flight for China.

That morning, while I was downstairs in our hotel tending to our luggage, I got to chatting with one of the fellows in our group and he told me this story. He had come on the trip with a supply of Scotch that he liked to "sample" prior to retiring. I guess he had hit it too hard and ran out. He went out and found a store that sold liquor. On entering he pointed to a bottle of Chivas Regal, costing $45 US, and presented his credit card. The girl behind the counter motioned that she would not take the credit card. As she was putting the bottle back on the shelf this guy heard someone beside him say something in Korean. With that the girl put the bottle in a bag and presented it to him. The Korean man next to him said "Korean buy." This fellow said he guessed the Korean to be about 35 years old. He was flabbergasted but accepted the gift, thanked him profusely, and left with his bottle of Scotch. Many of the Koreans, young and old, are very thankful for what we did there 50 years ago.

By the time we left for the airport Flo was feeling much better. This was due probably a combination of the medication the Army had supplied her and the sleep she had gotten the previous day. Many of our tour group were heading for the US and home.

At Kimpo we boarded our 747 and headed west for our 2-hour flight to Beijing, China. During one of our many bus rides our tour leader talked a little about North Korea. The tour company is trying to open up North Korea to tourism. This is what he had to say about that Communist "utopia." Every person in North Korea is issued a "rice card." This allows that person to get his ration of rice from the government. The card is valid as long as that person is contributing to society, working, going to school, or whatever. The card is only good in the general area where it was issued. So, if you are not contributing to society or have tried to leave your area for another your card is no longer valid and you get no rice. If there is no rice you don't eat and therefore you die. This is how the North Korean government controls it's populous. Scary, No?

EPILOGUE

RECENTLY I HAD been thinking about the Armed Forces and specifically about my experiences in the Air Force back sooo many years ago. My thoughts revolved about how fouled up the service seems sometimes. But then I got to thinking of my situation specifically. Maybe they weren't as confused as I thought they were.

What I am getting at is they, the higher ups, knew exactly where I was, what I was doing, and just when I was to be sent home for discharge. Me, just one measly little individual.

When you really think about all that goes on in the service, any branch, how they take care of the individuals is quite amazing.